Becoming an Outstanding Languages Teacher

Becoming an Outstanding Languages Teacher explores the skills that it takes to deliver exceptional language teaching and produce outstanding results. Offering support to all language teachers, this book provides a wide range of approaches to teaching and learning that will help to keep students stimulated and engaged when studying languages.

Focusing on the nuts and bolts of lessons and teaching sequences, this guide looks at the methods used by teachers to engage their students and offers practical strategies and ideas on how to incorporate skilled questioning and other interactions into the classroom.

Drawing on a range of activities, case studies and tech tips to maximise engagement and learning, this book covers:

- running a room

- dissecting a lesson: written texts, visuals and task-based approaches

- enjoying sounds

- dissecting a lesson: speaking and writing

- purposeful games

- getting grammatical

- words and chunks

- teaching all abilities

- pace, questioning and other interactions

- moving them forwards.

Packed full of strategies that are easy to implement, this timely new book is essential reading for both trainee and practising language teachers.

Steve Smith taught languages for over 30 years and is former Head of Modern Languages at Ripon Grammar School, UK. He now writes and presents for the AQA examination board in England and works with both trainee teachers and authors through frenchteacher.net, an online teaching resource widely used around the world. He is also author of Language Teacher Toolkit, a popular blog about language teaching methodology (frenchteachernet.blogspot.co.uk).

Becoming an Outstanding Teacher
Series Editor: Jayne Bartlett

Becoming an Outstanding Languages Teacher
Steve Smith

Becoming an Outstanding English Teacher
Kate Sida-Nicholls

Becoming an Outstanding Mathematics Teacher
Jayne Bartlett

Becoming an Outstanding Languages Teacher

Steve Smith

Routledge
Taylor & Francis Group

LONDON AND NEW YORK

First published 2018
by Routledge

2 Park Square, Milton Park, Abingdon, Oxon OX14 4RN
and by Routledge
711 Third Avenue, New York, NY 10017

Routledge is an imprint of the Taylor & Francis Group, an informa business

British Library Cataloguing in Publication Data
A catalogue record for this book is available from the British Library

Library of Congress Cataloging in Publication Data
A catalog record for this book has been requested

ISBN: 978-1-138-05662-6 (hbk)
ISBN: 978-1-138-05663-3 (pbk)
ISBN: 978-1-315-16520-2 (ebk)

Typeset in Melior
by Saxon Graphics Ltd, Derby

Contents

Contents

List of Boxes

List of Boxes

List of Tables

List of Figures

Acknowledgements

I'm grateful to a number of teachers who have provided input and ideas for this book, notably Tom Bennett, Martina Bex, Gianfranco Conti, Joe Dale, Pauline Galea, Cécile Genneviève, Jake Hunton, Chris Lowe, Jess Lund, Barry Smith, Rachel Smith, Anne Swainston and Carrie Toth. Most of the content is based on my own experience and that gained observing many skilled colleagues over the years. I especially thank my wife Professor Elspeth Jones for proof-reading and commenting on the text.

Introduction

"We really like Miss Jones's lessons"; "We get loads done with Mr Davies"; "Mrs Brown is a legend – I've learned so much from her". Teachers would be happy to hear their students say these things, and they often do. Teaching languages is a hugely challenging but rewarding job and we all want to do it as well as we can. If you want to be the best language teacher that you can, this book is written for you. What do you have to do for students to value your work highly and to maximise their progress?

Let's be clear from the outset that it's impossible to clearly define an "outstanding" teacher. So much in our craft depends on relationships, the context of a school and the personal experience of the teacher. Circumstances vary to such a degree that there's no single recipe for great language teaching, but I'll do my best to show you in some detail my own perspective about how you might get the best from your students. What you'll read is mainly based on my own long experience, together with what I observed in my talented colleagues' lessons and what I've picked up from my own reading. Other teachers would offer quite different perspectives; indeed, the final chapter of the book features descriptions of some quite unorthodox ways teachers produce impressive results.

What's different about this handbook compared to others I've read is that it drills down a good deal more into the nuts and bolts of lesson planning. I'll describe, almost line by line, how to work with a text or a set of pictures, for example. I'll be looking at the types of interactions you can use, how you can successfully sequence activities, how to give students the best chance of remembering language and using it for themselves. Even if you don't agree with every aspect of what you'll read, you should find that it challenges you to think about your own practice and become even better.

We never have enough time with our students, so we can't afford to waste the time we get with them. You'll discover my preference for working at pace, making every activity useful, avoiding fun for the sake of it and fostering an enjoyable environment where learning is at the forefront. It's a great feeling when you know a class is progressing fast and working hard for you. How can you make this happen?

You'll discover too that I place great value on providing as much target language input as possible in a structured and meaningful fashion. I believe you can learn skills through presentation and practice, careful scaffolding of activities and building up from the simple to the more complex. You'll also see that I favour an eclectic mix of teacher-led lessons, pair work, varied tasks, all with the aim of recycling language in as many ways as possible.

You could read the book from cover to cover or just dip in and out, using specific chapters to help shape your practice for individual lessons. There are plenty of ready-made activities you can lift and use with confidence, adapting them to your classes as necessary.

To save space I'll use "TL" for target language and so that teachers of all languages follow my examples I'll use English sources most of the time. You'll easily be able to adapt the examples to the languages you teach. I'll include a brief list of references for further reading at the end. These are books and blogs I've found particularly useful in shaping my thinking.

I hope you find the book a useful resource in becoming an outstanding language teacher.

Steve Smith

Chapter 1

Running a room

Starts and ends of lessons

Jane is an outstanding teacher.

Before the lesson begins her students are lining up outside the classroom. They're quiet or talking calmly. She stands by the doorway as they enter in single file. She says *bonjour* to each student. Because her school has a clear uniform code, she sometimes has the odd word with them about their appearance, maybe a little *ça va?* a bit of personal chit-chat in English here and there: "What lesson have you had? How was it?" "How did that piano exam go?" "Did you watch that football game?" She shows that she knows something about each student and knows them all by name. She asks them to use some French they recently learned as their entry code.

Her classroom is all ready to go. It's bright, at the right temperature, decorated with samples of student work, some useful French phrases, some positive behaviour statements, a map of France and a few posters showing aspects of French culture. There's a reading corner with a selection of French magazines and on each student table a mini-whiteboard and tissue. The computer, CD/MP3 player and interactive whiteboard are fired up and raring to go. On her desk there's a pile of marked exercise books waiting to be handed out.

The class is now in the room having taken out their materials. They're calmly standing behind their tables, facing the front (because they can see the teacher better that way). Jane is standing front middle and expects total silence at this point. She's smiling, communicating relaxed vigilance to the class. She scans the room from left to right, front to back, then greets the class with a *Bonjour tout le monde!* They reply in unison *Bonjour, madame.* She asks how they all are and they reply in unison *Ça va bien merci, et vous?* She says *Asseyez-vous.* She asks them to hold up their equipment: *pencil case, workbook, pen.* They do so in unison. The students sit down in their allocated places in a pattern and listen attentively to what she's going to say next. She can immediately see who's absent and makes a note.

That may all seem very familiar to you, but routines like this don't just happen. You can have that start to every lesson by modelling and practising all the desired behaviours and especially if your school's ethos supports best behaviour. Students have to learn routines, they like them and teachers have to practise them until students get them right. Be insistent, persevere and don't accept second best. Use eye contact, make sure the students know you're looking at them as individuals, preferably with a smile – a smile communicates confidence. Definitely smile before Christmas.

The first few minutes of a lesson are critical. In the real world, lessons don't always start perfectly, but you can help the process along with a trick or two. With younger classes you can tell them you're going to count down in the TL from 20 to zero and that they must have all their materials out by the time you get to zero (you can adjust your speed to the class). Or why not have the class recite or sing the alphabet as they come in and they have to have all their books ready by the time they get to Z? When it comes to the class sitting down, you could occasionally break the routine by saying they can sit down when they hear the first letter of their name. Students like to know what they should do, they appreciate clarity and feel safe with routines, as do you.

The mood of a class when it arrives partly depends on the previous lesson. If they've been quiet for an hour they may feel like being noisier now. If they've been allowed to be too noisy in the previous class this could carry over to your lesson. The outstanding teacher is aware of these subtle, or not so subtle, changing moods and adapts to them.

What if you get latecomers? In most cases you don't need to make a fuss; you can defer any individual comment until later to focus on your priority, getting the lesson off to a great start. Make sure the class has seen you've noticed the latecomer. Perhaps you've taught them to say *Excusez-moi, je suis en retard.* Just occasionally you may need to make a big fuss, show real or feigned disapproval. In this way the rest of the class knows that you don't accept lateness and that they may feel foolish if late. This isn't being mean to students; it's showing them how much you care. If a whole class is late for no good reason you may need to have them back at break or lunchtime to make your point.

Some teachers prefer to have a task ready on the board or on students' tables for them to do straight away. This may work well, especially if students arrive in dribs and drabs, but in general I'd go for a whole group activity to set the tone, give lesson objectives and have everyone in the same mindset. Worksheets are best placed face down on tables if you intend to use them later. If you hand out sheets during a lesson do it while walking round talking about something else so you minimise 'dead time'.

Ends of lessons need tidy routines as well. You can use a song as you did at the start to minimise any time-wasting chit-chat. Have all the students stand up. Try to end the lesson on a positive note, e.g. by mentioning a good website you came across, giving a compliment to one of the students or even telling an amusing story. Then you can end with a *Rangez vos affaires* or equivalent and ask the class to stand up together. To ensure an orderly departure you can let them out in rows or boys first, then girls (or vice versa). Even that last trick makes the class listen to whether you're going to say *boys* or *girls* first. They'll soon let you know if you're favouring one group over the other!

Make sure you leave enough time for your end routine. It's very easy to be too rushed. If you need to fill time, individual students can use an exit code, e.g. a phrase they've learned recently, a verb form, a time or a weather phrase. Give yourself and your class plenty of time to write down any homework – you don't want students telling you next time that they weren't sure what to do. Some say you should set the homework earlier in the lesson; that's great if the lesson sequence allows for it.

Planning lesson sequences

You hopefully have a well-organised scheme of work or curriculum plan in your department. It's both difficult and unwise to plan every lesson too far in advance because you have to adapt to the pace and the needs of the class in front of you and they're all different. Most teachers make a broad plan for weeks ahead, but prepare detailed lessons a week or two in advance. Last minute preparation isn't advised, but it happens and can produce fresh, successful lessons. This gets easier with experience and excellent teachers are great improvisers. Over a sequence of lessons try to mix up the skills you're going to practise. Allow for some reading, listening, speaking and writing. Remember that students become good at what you practise. If you do lots of oral work they'll probably get better at oral work; if you do lots of grammar, they'll get good at grammar, and so on. Research suggests that meaningful input and interaction are the key recipes for success.

Think about the timing of your lessons with the class. Plan for a greater amount of "passive" work like listening, gap-filling, dictation, computer work and reading in the afternoons. The students are tired, so are you; you may find it hard to get a class going for oral work. Conversely, morning lessons may be better for a larger diet of oral work (pair work, group work, question and answer, other teacher-student interactions, repetition and games). Be flexible, though. Great teachers sometimes change what they'd planned to do if the mood of the class is not as expected. There's no doubt that feeling the class mood and having a degree of flexibility are important attributes. We'll look at this in more detail later.

Over a sequence of lessons, plan to recycle language from one lesson to the next. Your start to the lesson might be a quick recap of a grammar point or some vocabulary from the previous lesson: "Who thinks they can remember five shops in Spanish?" "Who thinks they can go through the verb *fahren* for me?" (Note that adding the word "think" makes the task seem less intimidating to students.) Or: "I'll give you the name of a food item, put your hand up and tell me if you think you should put *du, de la* or *des* in front of it". "I'll give you a sentence in the present tense, you try to put it in the past and change one item." But don't just revise from the previous lesson, go back over various things you've done in the last few lessons. You'll find no shortage of ideas for starters in course books, online or from colleagues. Remember that many students' memories are nowhere near as good as yours. The use of spaced learning or "little and often" is essential for language teachers.

Planning individual lessons

If you have one-hour or even two-hour lessons, you need to build in plenty of variety. The attention span of youngsters is often quite short. In a one-hour session you might include four, five or more different tasks. It's usually best to put oral work nearer the start, when students have more energy. It's a good idea to set short time targets to create a sense of urgency: *Vous avez cinq minutes*. Break up the pattern of oral work by moving between whole-class question and answer and bursts of pair work. The latter is easier to manage than group work and each student gets to speak more.

Make sure that students know what you intend to get done in the lesson (usually in English) and what the outcomes will be for them. "By the end of the lesson you'll be able to…" This doesn't necessarily mean writing up the objectives on the board. You don't need to spell out objectives at the very start; you may prefer to get straight into your starter or main task, then spell out the aims later. Why not invite the class to work out what the aim of the lesson is?

Great teachers make sure each task follows on logically from the previous one, constantly reinforcing the main learning points. You may only be working on one or two key areas in a whole lesson. To maximise the recycling of language you can repeat tasks in slightly different ways. You might do a task from a worksheet or the board orally and then get the class to do the same task in writing. This leads to a quick transition, reinforces previous learning and practises more than one skill.

Be crystal clear with instructions, perhaps checking with the class that they've understood. Say in English: "Who can explain what we've been doing?" Don't use a questioning intonation when you give an instruction. Students are quite happy to be told what to do firmly and politely.

Try to ensure tidy, prompt transitions from one task to the next. This can be a tough one, especially for inexperienced teachers. When you stop one task there is a natural release of tension and students may start talking off the subject at that point. You may actually want a little of that, because it acts as a "pause for breath" before the next task. On the whole, however, it wastes valuable time and you have to work at transitions just like you have to work at starts and ends. Bring the class to silence with a familiar noise, a firm clap, a bell, a countdown or just by raising your arm, telling students they have to raise their arms too when silence is needed. Try saying "Class" with a particular sing-song intonation which students get used to and even copy. Tell the class why it's important to have a quick transition. Let them into your thinking, making them part of the process. If you have a reward system, why not tell them that the first three to finish will get a merit/stamp/house points, etc?

Try to mix up your interaction styles with the class. Don't talk *too* much to them, they'll probably get bored and learn less, but don't forget that teacher talk is important because it supplies high-quality TL input at the right speed, tailor-made for the class and you may have interesting stories to tell which increase their cultural awareness. Elicit responses, ask for hands up and sometimes say that you're going to just select students to answer. The no hands up technique, favoured by many, is a controversial one since we don't want to make students uncomfortable with language learning, or even terrified, yet we do need to ensure they're concentrating. If you use the no hands up technique sparingly it can work well. The class comes to attention and you just need to ensure that you don't throw an impossibly hard question to a student.

I'd argue against random questioning, using lolly sticks with names on or digital spinners, for example, since I believe the teacher is the best judge of who to ask at any point and how to differentiate between students by using skilled questioning. But you have to be careful – research suggests teachers find it hard not to favour the confident students with their hands in the air. If you want to ensure all students are joining in, sometimes get them to write their answers on a mini-whiteboard, allowing them some more thinking time and you to see their responses.

I'd advocate using pair work a lot when you're confident the class will do it usefully. Use games when they have a clear learning goal and you're sure students won't abuse the situation. Your lesson doesn't need to be "fun". It's great when you're having fun, but the main aim is for students to be engaged in cognitively stimulating and therefore enjoyable activity. Games with a clear learning purpose are described in Chapter 6.

Use technology if you're confident with it. Teachers sometimes report that students who aren't very comfortable learning a language will be more at ease and learn more with a screen and microphone in front of them. Technology is great for us language teachers and you may choose to use it a good deal, but any digital task needs to be linguistically useful, providing high-quality input or practice opportunities. You'll find technology tips at the end of most of the chapters of this book.

When you start teaching you'll need to write out your lesson plan in some detail, preparing exactly which questions you're going to ask, how you're going to drill an item, how you're going to mix, say, group repetition with individual oral work. This takes time and care. With more experience these skills become second nature and your preparation is less time consuming, allowing you to focus on other areas of your professional life. The "dissecting a lesson" chapters in this book give examples of interactions you can plan for in detail.

Last of all, assessment for learning (formative assessment) techniques are important (see Chapters 12 and 13): checking all the class is following, using mini-whiteboards, skilled questioning techniques and the rest, but your personality counts for a lot. Children want you to be firm, friendly and fair. They want to be supported, so when someone is stuck, you can engender a supportive atmosphere by saying "Can anyone help her?" Let's now look at some useful lesson starters.

Great lesson starters activities

Starters or "warmers" get the class in the right mood, help you manage your classroom, but, above all, are an effective way to recycle language, providing students with more TL input and practice. Having a flying start sets the tone for the whole lesson. You can do random starters, but it's better if they fit within your individual lesson or lesson sequence, complementing other activities, either recapping material from the previous lesson or prefacing the content of the lesson to follow.

Box 1.1: Starters for beginners

Guess the flashcard

You hold about ten flashcards in your hand so the class can't see them. The words on the cards have been practised in the previous lesson. You then choose one and ask the class to guess what it is. Younger learners enjoy guessing games and you can spice up the task by making pauses before you reveal the answer or by pretending you're going to say "Yes", then let them down with a "No". A student can take over leading the activity. A five-minute starter of this type will generate multiple uses of the target words, helping to embed them in the students' long-term memories.

What am I thinking of?

Similar to the above, if you've been working on a vocabulary topic just ask students to guess which word you're thinking of. You might be surprised how keen students are to make guesses.

Guess the word

You write a word on the board. Students have to guess what you're writing before you finish. Award a point to the class if they do and a point to yourself if they fail to guess the word before the end. Alternatively do this as a team game.

Mental maths

Read out a simple sum in TL while the students figure out the answer. They can either do this in their heads and write down the answer, or just write down each number as you go along. You should start with an easy example, then make them progressively harder depending on the ability of the class.

Box 1.2: Starters for intermediates

Word combining

Focusing on vocabulary you've been using in recent lessons, display three words, one a verb, to the whole class and get them to write down as many sentences as they can including the two words to a four-minute time limit. You can then listen back to some of their sentences or, more productively if the mood is right, get the students to compare their answers in pairs.

Detect my lies

Display and read aloud ten numbered TL statements about yourself, half of which are true, the other half lies. Ask the class to try to identify the lies. You could include some outrageously untrue statements as well as some more plausible ones. Then reveal the true and false answers. With the right class this could then be handed over to students to make up their own list for a partner to guess from.

Two-minute topics

Write some topics you've been teaching on cards, e.g. family, hobbies, home town, last weekend, and give them to students face down in the middle of the table. Organise pairs or small groups. One student picks up a card and the group talk about the topic for two minutes, then another student picks up another card and changes the topic.

Box 1.3: Starters for advanced students

Lateral thinking stories

You present a scenario and the students have to find out what happened using only yes/no questions. Here are three examples:

1   When Jack comes home he finds Mandy is dead, lying in a pool of water and Tom is sitting quietly on the armchair. There's some broken glass on the floor. Tom won't be charged with murder. Why not? **Answer:** Mandy is a fish and Tom is a cat. Mandy was swimming in her bowl. Tom started playing with it and knocked it over.
2   A woman lives on the 30th floor of a building. When she gets home from work, she usually takes the lift as far as the 21st floor and then climbs the stairs to the 30th. However when it's raining, she'll always take the lift to the 30th floor. What explains this strange behaviour? **Answer:** She's of small stature and can't reach the top button unless she's carrying an umbrella.
3   A man sprints up some stairs, desperately turns on a light switch, looks out of the window and sees dead people everywhere, then commits suicide. Why does he do this? **Answer:** He was the operator of a lighthouse and forgot to switch on the light.

Tube train

This is really a twist on speed dating. You line up two rows of chairs, facing each other and all quite close together. Each student sits down, facing their partner and all students are given a topic to discuss with each other for two minutes. Then one student moves along the train, all the students should have a new partner and the game begins again, this time with a new topic. Another way to do this is to have students sit or stand in two concentric circles.

Just a minute

In small groups each student has to talk for a minute on a subject of their choosing, while the other students check the time. If the student hesitates badly another student "buzzes in" and takes over the topic for the rest of the minute. You can choose topics for the students, preferably linking up with recent work.

Persuade a partner yours is better

Get the students to all write down their favourite film. In small groups they then have to persuade the other people that their choice is more important than the others. Students can repeat this with their favourite animal, TV programme, social media platform, etc.

Seating plans

Effective teachers nearly always have a seating plan which can later be adjusted depending on the behaviour of individual students. Consider a boy-girl plan to encourage best behaviour. Why not change your seating plan every now and again? If students always work with the same partner they'll always hear the same accent, the same errors, always be in the comfort zone and maybe not do enough work. Saying "Now go and work with someone you don't know very well" freshens up lessons and gets students to put in a bit more effort. Some students just need to sit apart from each other for their own good.

To learn names you could either draw your seating plan out, use a digital planner, or get the students to make name plates which they put on their desk for the first few lessons. Many teachers take a photo of the class or individual students for their planner. As you walk around the class in the early days try to memorise names by looking at exercise books. When handing these out, get students to put up their hand when you call their name. Great teachers get to know their students quickly.

Correcting

How much should I correct? In class oral work you need to find a balance. You may allow your quickest student to answer first to give a good model, but be prepared occasionally to use the no hands up ("cold-calling") technique to make sure all students are alert and ready to respond. If someone makes an error, usually correct with a positive tone. Use the "return to student" technique, i.e. if a student makes a mistake or can't answer, go to other students, then return to the original student so they have a chance to respond well without your help. When it comes to pronunciation errors, make the whole idea of pronouncing accurately fun. Try to get students to enjoy making those strange sounds. Use "backward repetition", e.g. in French a student says "natashion" instead of "natation". Get the whole class to say "on", then "ion", then "tion", then "ation", then "tation", then "atation", then the whole word. Then get the first student to say the word. Try speaking English with an amusing TL accent; get students to do the same just to enjoy the sounds. For more on enjoying sounds, see Chapter 5. Research into error correction provides no clear answers, but most good teachers do selectively correct and provide "recasts", i.e. corrected versions of the student's response. I'd go along with this since recasts provide more input for the student and show other students who heard an error what the corrected version should be.

How much target language?

Language teachers talk a lot about this and it's fair to say that opinions vary! I'll put this as simply as I can: students need to hear lots of the TL (what's sometimes called in the second language acquisition jargon "comprehensible input") to allow their brains to exploit their natural language-learning capability and for language to enter long-term memory. But students also need to develop a relationship with you and clearly understand what they have to do in a lesson. So my rule of thumb would be to use the TL most of the time, maybe in chunks of ten minutes or so, then release tension with some English. Try not to constantly "echo", by which I mean don't use a bit of TL then instantly translate it into English. Why would a student bother to listen to the TL if they know you're going to translate it all the time?

Remember that even experienced teachers tend to overestimate how much a student understands in the TL. You'd be wise, therefore, to use English occasionally to make sure everyone knows what's going on and to get feedback. Some argue for lots of translation for this very reason, but I'd argue against this point of view since it's bound to reduce the overall amount of input the students receive. Whatever you do, don't lose the class! Students often report that their interest flags when the teacher doesn't use English enough. Match your use of TL to the needs of the class, but try to use as much of it as you can. Don't get lazy about it just because it seems easier at the time.

Ultimately the amount of TL used depends on the quality of the lesson planning. A well thought-through lesson with good support via gestures, physical objects and other visual aids will allow you to use lots of the TL with nearly every class. Exploit mime, flashcards, pictures, PowerPoint, written words on the board – whatever it takes. We'll dig down into this in greater detail in subsequent chapters, particularly Chapters 2, 3, 4, 9, and 10.

Vary the teaching mode

Language learning is demanding on the ears and eyes, but you can mix up your planning to include gesture, body movement, drawing and song ("Simon Says" is a super whole-body game which works with all ages – see Chapter 6). If you value chanting verb paradigms, get classes to do so while pointing in different directions for the various persons of the verb – sideways for third person, forwards for second person and so on. You can sing them too; use the Mission Impossible theme for –ar verbs in Spanish or Here We Go Round the Mulberry Bush for avoir in French.

Students can spell out words in the air with their fingers or noses. Get them to move around the class looking for words you've stuck on walls. Get them to come up to the front and use the board. Let them play teacher from time to time. Have them jump up and down while singing the alphabet to an American marines marching song. Get one student to draw while their partner describes. Even using a computer, tablet or mini-whiteboard allows a fidgety child to be busy with their hands. Mathematical children may particularly enjoy number games and code-breaking vocabulary games. Musical children may enjoy singing. Artistic children may like making posters or drawing on the board.

Keeping them on task

Creating a successful learning environment is the number one priority for teachers of any level of experience. Learning won't occur if students are inattentive and misbehaving. Where behaviour is already good and supported by an excellent school ethos and behaviour policy, the challenge is to stretch classes to the limit with engaging and challenging activities. Many classes, however, take a good deal more management, and effective teachers use a range of strategies to generate the right environment. A detailed discussion of behaviour management is beyond the scope of this book, but I can't stress enough that this is the key priority in teaching and obviously a major concern for those new to the profession. I would recommend any teacher to read *Classroom Behaviour* by Bill Rogers (2015) and *Teach Like a Champion* 2.0 by Doug Lemov (2015).

Elements of good classroom management are neatly summed up by teacher and writer Tom Bennett in Text Box 1.4.

Box 1.4: Three Rs of classroom management

Routines: embedding habits of conduct and learning to maximise the good of both without the need to constantly create them on the spot. This means rules and consequences, but also "micro-behaviours" like how to scaffold essays, work in groups, or speak to a visitor.

Responses: the strategies that work best to restore order, promote a return to learning and deal with crises when they occur.

Relationships: interpersonal skills, body language for example, but also the appropriate use of prior data, personal well-being, and working with parents, carers, etc. These are intimately tied up with cognitive and affective empathy.

Great teachers often use humour and a competitive element, e.g. dividing the class into teams for activities. They respect every student in the class, act promptly on low-level disruption, minimise confrontation by taking the sting out of situations, and show empathy with students, grasping what they may be finding hard or threatening. They use eye contact and facial expression to communicate feeling, employ techniques such as tactical pausing and take-up time (allowing students to take in an instruction before they act on it). They rarely shout; indeed they may speak deliberately quietly to gain more attention. They're well organised, business-like and punctual. They're not overbearing, but employ what can be termed "relaxed vigilance".

They make effective use of their physical presence, e.g. they don't always stand or sit in the same place in the classroom. They move to the back when all the class is focused on reading aloud from the board, creating the feeling that the class and teacher are working together. They sometimes place themselves near unsettled students or they gently move towards students who may be at risk of going off-task, having a quiet word in their ear rather than making a fuss in front of the class. But they don't create a distraction by moving around too much.

Great teachers sometimes award points or certificates for positive behaviour and achievement, tracking them over a period of time. They don't praise in a routine way, but selectively and often confidentially, beyond the hearing of the class. They always show respect and never belittle any student. If they feel the need to criticise a class for poor behaviour or work, they quickly move on in a positive manner. They try not to let a bad lesson get them down; the students will forget it more quickly than the teacher. They're usually "authentic", i.e. when they show disappointment, anger or pleasure it's because these feelings are genuinely felt. In general, they have a "no excuses" attitude, but with a degree of flexibility, showing that they care by expecting the highest standards.

The best teachers are aware of motivational theories such as self-efficacy, i.e. the strength of one's belief in the ability to complete tasks and reach goals. They manage to create in their students the self-belief they need to persist with activities. They do everything they can to build confidence and remove anxiety in students. Equally, they know how much students are driven by instrumental goals, e.g. getting a good grade in the exam, as well as, for some, integrative goals such as wanting to be part of the TL culture and community.

A sense of responsibility and pride can be engendered in students in a number of ways, e.g. as we've seen, you can get individuals to lead the class, or they can run a club, teach a partner or a younger student. You can send a postcard home to parents praising an achievement, relay a message to a class tutor or nominate someone "student of the month". You can use exercise books as a privileged, confidential means of communication, praising or requesting improvement where needed. You can write a personal note to students and request a reply. Class exchanges, study trips, Skype sessions, Facebook groups and email exchanges can all enhance students' integrative motivation.

Crucially, an effective teacher has highly developed empathy skills. What does this mean?

Cognitive empathy

This is the capacity to understand another's perspective or mental state. In teaching we can say that it refers to the teacher's ability to marry every level of their teaching (e.g. planning lessons, classroom delivery, feedback provision, target setting, homework) to their students' thinking processes. We could break it down as follows:

1) **An awareness of the cognitive challenges** posed by language learning in general and by the specific language items you're teaching. For example, knowing that the learning of adjective agreement is tough for English-speaking students because the concept doesn't exist in English; or anticipating that direct and indirect object pronouns in French will be especially hard because of the word order problems they create; or being aware of the challenges posed by the German case system.

2) **An understanding of how students respond to such challenges**. This involves an awareness of how cognition in a language-learning context is affected by individual variables, e.g. age group, gender, personality type, culture, etc. For example, younger students usually find it harder than older ones to apply grammatical rules taught explicitly. Some topics appeal to some groups more than others, depending on the make-up and background of the class.

Affective empathy

Also called "emotional intelligence", this is the capacity to respond with an appropriate emotion to another's affective state. For the teacher, this can work at a whole-class level (having a feel for the general mood) or at an individual level (sensing at any moment how a student might be reacting emotionally to the task they're doing).

Effective teachers seem either to do these things instinctively (the so-called "natural teacher") or have learned to exercise them through reading, training or experience. Teachers who begin their careers very successfully enhance their skills with time and deliberate practice, while others who initially find the classroom hard can turn into excellent practitioners.

Learning aspects of cognitive empathy is easier for most teachers than mastering affective empathy, since you can, by contrasting English and the TL, anticipate what will be easier and harder. For example, adjectival agreement, gender and tense usage are bound to be issues for English-speaking learners of European languages. A sound knowledge of second-language teaching methodology is also easy to acquire, namely understanding the principles of natural language acquisition and second-language acquisition theories.

Showing social and emotional intelligence requires observing and listening to students carefully, picking up any visual or spoken clues to their mood and detecting any relationship patterns between students. You can help the process along by effective assessment for learning (formative assessment) techniques, e.g. asking students how they feel about what they've learned, what their attitudes are to language learning, specific activity types and non-English-speaking cultures. Teachers with well-developed cognitive and affective empathy are able to avoid confrontation, be positive, make students feel cared for and self-assured, while not becoming over-anxious when things don't go as planned. Anxiety spreads anxiety. Some teachers are, of course, more compassionate than others but, in general, the more a teacher is able to look out to others rather than look in to themselves, the better.

It comes down to something Bill Rogers (2015) has written about: when students talk about their teachers they may mention subject-related matters, but they're more likely to talk about the kind of teacher they have, whether they teach well and interestingly, and whether they're fair, considerate, patient and have a sense of humour. Above all they talk about whether their teachers care.

Box 1.5: Tech tips

You don't have to use digital technology (tech) tools to be an excellent teacher, but they offer a wide range of ways to enhance lessons. Digital tech can be seamlessly integrated into lessons, allowing you to listen to material recorded by students, set work and give quick feedback as it comes in, administer quick quizzes, allow Special Educational Needs and Disabilities (SEND) students the chance to produce work without writing or typing, do interactive grammar tasks, keep a flow of work going for absentees, create tailor-made text books, share students' work with the whole world, or within a closed group, and produce exciting presentational materials. At the end of each chapter I'll refer to some popular examples of technology used to great effect.

If you're new to tech it may be wise to start with one or two tools and become proficient with them before moving on. A good start would be to become skilled with all the possibilities presented by the **interactive whiteboard** (IWB).

With apps and other tech tools, bear in mind whether the activity is worth the return on investment of time. Advanced level students will use some productive apps more efficiently than younger students. You may find that some apps are more useful to you as a creative tool than they are for students who may end up spending too much time on non-linguistic activity. Just because a student likes an activity doesn't mean it's their best use of time.

Any specific programs or apps referred to were available in 2017.

ClassDojo is a widely used behaviour management tool. Each student has a profile – complete with their own avatar – to which you can attach positive and negative points ("dojos") throughout the lesson. The program can be operated from a smartphone, tablet or computer, and each time you award a point an (optional) sound plays to alert the class. This information is recorded on students' profiles so that it can be reviewed throughout the year. Parents also have logins so that they can view their child's achievements from home.

Edmodo is a web-based platform that provides a safe and easy way for your class to connect and collaborate, share content, and access homework, grades and school notices. It's like Facebook but in a secure and controlled environment appropriate for school. It provides a secure environment where you can create a classroom group for your students. There is an option for parents to access the platform. In this virtual group you can:

- place digital resources for students to access or download;

- create polls for students to vote online;

- write short summaries of lessons for students who were absent from class (better yet, get your students to write the summary);

- post homework information.

iDoceo is an app which you can use as a planner, mark book, class seating planner, diary and resources manager. You can also send resources or reports to students by email.

Too Noisy is an app designed to help you keep control of general noise levels in a classroom. As the noise in a classroom increases beyond an acceptable level the noise level meter indicates the level and the graphics within the app change to reflect the noise levels. You can control the sensitivity of the app by using a slider so the app can be used for all types of lessons. It can be displayed on an iPad and the IWB.

Concluding remarks

You'll often hear teachers say that the key to success in the classroom is establishing a good rapport with classes. This is quite true, but a great relationship alone is no guarantee of the very best outcomes. Subject knowledge, skilful planning and execution of lessons, awareness of pedagogical approaches and, as we've seen, a basic knowledge of second-language acquisition theory are also important elements when it comes to getting the very best out of students. The rest of the book will examine in some detail a number of these areas, while Chapter 14 will attempt to distil these various elements. In the next chapter we'll begin the process of dissecting lessons and analysing effective practice. What do you have to do in your lessons for students to really value your work?

CHAPTER 2

Dissecting a lesson: visuals

Introduction

This is the first chapter of a number that will examine in detail how you can work through lesson sequences in the classroom. The emphasis will be on the specific interactions between you and students, as well as between students themselves.

The rationale for using pictures and other visual aids is that they make language more memorable, provide an excellent focus of attention and enable you to teach without too much recourse to English. In this chapter I'll examine in detail how you can exploit pictures to the best effect. I'll break down suggested teaching routines with the aim of highlighting how effective teachers generate intensive input and output-rich language. These types of teaching sequence are characteristic of the oral-situational approach, one type of communicative language teaching.

Exploiting flashcards with beginners

Suppose that your aim is to introduce the vocabulary associated with places around town with **beginners**. Your target vocabulary might be 12 items in the first lesson – you can adapt this number depending on the class's ability: *swimming pool, supermarket, town hall, park, car park, cinema, museum, theatre, bank, restaurant, café, market.*

For each of the vocabulary items you have a large, clear hand-held flashcard with the word spelled out at the bottom so that students can immediately associate the picture with both the sound and the spelling of the word. You separate out the items by gender, teaching items of the same gender together. Table 2.1 describes a suggested teaching sequence with a commentary. Target language is italicised.

By the end of the sequence described in Table 2.1, students have heard each item numerous times, you've been speaking almost entirely in the TL and every student has uttered the words repeatedly, either individually or chorally. There's been some fun and amusement along the way, with the class hearing accurate and

Table 2.1 Exploiting hand-held flashcards (1)

Teacher	Student(s)	Commentary
Here is the cinema. *Here is the park.* *Here is the market.* – all 12 items. (Do this all twice.)	Listening and watching.	Students just listen as you say each word. Students need time to hear and take in the new sounds. No need to force any repetition.
The cinema. *The park.* *The market,* etc – all 12 items.	*The cinema* (x2). *The park* (x2). *The market* (x2).	Choral repetition, focusing on accurate pronunciation, exaggerating vowel and consonant sounds a little. No need to rush. You could vary the repetition style by whispering.
What's this? It's the cinema (x2).	Listening and watching?	Allow students to hear the question and the answer.
What's this? (show a card) (x12).	Hands up. *It's the cinema,* etc.	Elicit answers from volunteers with hands up. Get other individuals to repeat the correct answer. Get the whole class to repeat correct answers.
Either/or questions, e.g. *Is this the cinema or the market?*	*It's the cinema.*	You can create a comic effect by stressing the right answer in each pair or by refusing to accept their option, e.g. *No, it's not the cinema!*
Hide all the cards. Ask in English how many the class can remember.	Hands up. *The cinema,* etc.	Elicit suggestions with hands up. Try to obtain all 12 items.
Ask in English who can list all 12 on their own.	Hands up. *The cinema, the park, the café,* etc.	You can prompt the student by giving the first sound or syllable of a word. If a student is struggling, encourage others to help out.
Play "hide the flashcard". Tell the class they have to guess the hidden card.	Hands up. Students make guesses.	You can add comic effect by pretending with a facial expression that they've got the answer right, then say no!

clear models of each word. A sequence such as this would take at most 15 minutes, after which time a "release of tension" or change of direction in the lesson is called for. You could, for example, have five minutes of quiet time, with students copying down the words with their definite articles. You may have prepared a simple set of similar pictures next to which the students can copy the words. If you get students to draw their own pictures, remember this takes time.

In the following lesson you could practise a pared-down version of the above sequence, allowing students to show off what they've remembered. To add interest, you could vary the interactions a little, e.g. you could hide a card and offer students a choice of three, thus speeding up the process while allowing them to hear the words again. You could then do a moving-around task where you pin on the walls of the class numbered pictures and supply students with a written, lettered list of the items. To a time limit students have to move round and find which letters match which numbers. Once you feel the students are ready to move on, you can then add a little more challenge by introducing the phrase *there is* (e.g. *In my town there is a cinema*). See Table 2.2.

After the sequence described in Table 2.2 a transition to a new task would make sense. You can display a brief written description of a town on the board, including the items you've practised and a few more, preferably cognates. Read aloud the description, then get the whole group to repeat a few words at a time after you. Insist on accurate pronunciation. Then put the students into pairs and tell them to read aloud the paragraph to their partner, encouraging partners to offer positive feedback on performance. Next give the opportunity for a few individual volunteers to perform their reading aloud in front of the class. (Beginners often enjoy reading aloud to their peers.)

You can imagine that a range of further reading and writing tasks could ensue, including ones that get a bit closer to the way the language is used in real-life situations, e.g. combining the names of places in the town with simple directions given from a map. The main point here has been to demonstrate how you can introduce and practise items repeatedly, with little pain, almost all in TL. Outstanding teachers are thorough about this type of activity, making it a positive and fun experience while making the most out of TL input and practice activities.

Exploiting PowerPoint slides with beginners

This section suggests how to get the best out of a typical set of PowerPoint slides with **beginners**, in this case with the aim of teaching classroom objects together with "I have": *J'ai, Tengo, Ich habe*. Your resource is a set of 39 slides laid out as below. For lower-attaining classes you could limit the number of slides somewhat.

Table 2.2 Exploiting hand-held flashcards (2)

Teacher	Student(s)	Commentary
You list a few items (maybe invented) of places in your town. *In my town there is a cinema* *In my town there is a swimming pool*, etc.	Listening and watching you.	Students take in the new sounds for "in my town" and "there is". Stress the difference in sounds between the different indefinite articles. Note that students will now be hearing the indefinite article, not the definite article they heard previously. This is fine, since at this stage they'll be starting to work out the difference between definite and indefinite articles.
You ask *What's in your town?* You can try this in TL, hoping students get the idea, or briefly say it in English first.	Hands up and no hands up. *A cinema.* *A park*, etc.	If there are errors of pronunciation or gender you can recast responses with the correct gender, making little fuss. The more you repeat them the more students will use the right gender instinctively. Think of how toddlers pick up gender in their first language.
Ask yes/no questions to allow students to hear the items again. *Is there a cinema?* *Is there a restaurant?* etc.	Yes/No (individual or choral depending on circumstances).	At any point you can always check understanding by asking students to translate a simple TL or English statement. You have to keep everyone on board.
Try to elicit longer answers, including more than one item. *What's in your town?*	Hands up and no hands up. *There is...*	Help the process along by offering the first sounds to get students going, e.g. *There is... There is...* Try eliciting a minimum number of responses.
"Who can list five things in their town?" (in English or TL)	Hands up and no hands up. *There is...*	Offer prompts if needed, then ask if anyone can do more than five, more than six, etc. Keep the whole class involved with occasional choral or individual repetition of answers.

French teachers can find it on *frenchteacher.net* as a free resource entitled Classroom Vocab. Teachers of other languages could easily adapt it.

- Eleven blue background slides featuring a masculine object with the phrase *J'ai un...* The article is in a different colour.

- Eight pink background slides featuring a feminine object with the phrase *J'ai une...* The article is in a different colour.

- Two slides each showing nine items of mixed gender with no accompanying words.

- Sixteen slides showing zoomed-in close-ups of a small part of each object.

The sequence in Table 2.3 once again lays the emphasis on recycling the vocabulary items numerous times, providing a large number of accurate models and the opportunity for students to speak either individually or as a group. You would conduct the activity at pace, keeping good eye contact with the class, using a remote slide controller and pointer if you have one.

I'd suggest returning to the same task (Table 2.3) in the next lesson, speeding up the sequence or altering it somewhat, perhaps focusing to a greater extent on the zoomed-in pictures you'll see on the slides. Alternatively you could reteach the same items using different slides or hand-held flashcards for the sake of variety. Effective teachers are skilled at adding a slight twist to a lesson so that students may feel they're doing something different while actually covering very similar ground. This is one way to ensure effective recycling and retention in long-term memory.

In passing, it's worth mentioning that some teachers are reluctant to carry out the type of task I've described, feeling that such parrot-like repetition forces students into speaking too soon and that there are other, more imaginative ways to introduce vocabulary. I'd argue that this approach combines speaking and listening, reinforces sound-letter relationships (phonics) and can be quite enjoyable. It also reinforces your central role as a leader on whom your students will want to depend. Doing these bread-and-butter tasks also helps to build your relationship with the class. You can use alternative strategies on other occasions, e.g. matching words to meaning by playing dominoes or translating, or letting students discover the words in the context of interesting authentic or adapted authentic texts.

Table 2.3 Exploiting PowerPoint slides

Teacher	Student(s)	Commentary
Show the first 11 slides while reading out each item. Just do the first nine slides, the masculine ones.	Listen and watch.	Check the students are all watching and listening carefully.
Repeat the sequence, getting the class to repeat chorally, e.g. *I have a pen.*	*I have a pen.*	Always insist on replies in unison. Listen for faulty pronunciation and fix it immediately. Otherwise errors may become fossilised, i.e. stay there for the long term.
Repeat the sequence once more.	Listen, watch and repeat chorally.	You can vary by using whispers or getting half the class to repeat at a time, e.g. boys and girls.
Repeat the above three steps with the feminine nouns (the next eight slides).	Listen, watch and repeat chorally.	Make the pronunciation of articles very clear.
Now you can show the two slides, each showing nine items. Point to an item and make either/or statements, e.g. *Have I got a pen or a ruler?*	(Hands up) *I have a ruler.* *I have a pencil case.* *I have a calculator,* etc.	There may be some gender confusion at this point, but by asking either/or questions you are allowing students to hear them again. This will embed the link between the article and the noun so that students learn the **whole chunk**, not just the noun in isolation. This is how they will retain the gender in the long term.
This time just ask the class *What do you have?* while pointing to items.	(Hands up and no hands up) *I have a pencil.* *I have a pencil sharpener,* etc.	The students get less input this time and have to provide the answer without being able to repeat. This will tell you if they've mastered the words and genders.
If the class is still attentive you can proceed to the zoomed-in close-ups on the slides and ask the same question *What do you have?*	(Hands up and no hands up) *I have a bag.* *I have a tablet,* etc.	You need to judge if the class has the focus to carry on at this point. Slower groups may need to return to this in the next lesson or later in the same lesson.

Figure 2.1 Picture sequence for storytelling

Table 2.4 Exploiting a storytelling picture sequence

Teacher	Commentary
Read out the description of your holiday depicted by the pictures. Key verbs, clearly enunciated, will include: *I left, I took, I went, I arrived, I ate, I took off, I travelled, I stayed, I visited, I went up, I did, I spent.*	You could run through this twice pointing at the relevant picture at each stage of the description. With more advanced classes you could add extra details for colour (perhaps using language recently practised in class), e.g. *what you ate* or *a brief description of the hotel.*
Tell students to imagine they went on this same holiday and you're going to ask them what happened. *What time did you leave?* *How did you get to the airport? By car? By bus?* etc.	Invite students to put their hands up. Recast ambiguous or incorrect answers. Get individuals to repeat good responses. Accept short answers with no verbs, then recast them with a verb and get them to repeat. As you proceed get faster students to put together a sequence of four pictures, then eight, then finally the whole sequence. This allows you to differentiate between students of different aptitudes.
Get students to recount the holiday to a partner.	Encourage fluency more than accuracy now. Tell students to support each other. If the class is good enough the same exercise can be repeated without reference to the pictures.
Tell the story again but with some deliberate errors thrown in. Tell the students to make a note in English or TL where there are errors.	Note-taking in TL is preferable, but not necessary if the class find this too hard. The focus here is mainly on listening comprehension.
Display a written version of the account. Read it aloud. Then display a gapped version of the same text.	Students have to fill the gaps, either writing them down or just giving oral responses.
Now remove all visual and written support. Read the account making pauses every now and then for students to add the next word or words.	You can adjust this task to the group. Some groups with excellent memories will be able to recall lots of words. With others you'll need to leave fewer gaps.
Move to a more analytical section of the lesson where you focus on the accuracy of past tense verb forms.	Students may want to ask questions in English at this point. This is a chance to check how much they've understood. Stress how well they've done to be able to understand and say so much, including some quite lengthy stretches of TL.

Exploiting a picture sequence with intermediate students

In this example for **low-intermediate** students who've studied a language for at least two or three years I'm going to analyse another example of "intensive input-output" activity. In this case the focus is on using the past (preterite) tense. You can tell students that by the end of the task they'll be able to understand someone talking about a holiday and describe one themselves. See Figure 2.1 and Table 2.4 for a suggested teaching sequence and a range of interactions you could use. You could present the pictures individually with PowerPoint first, but at some point there's a great advantage in making them all visible at the same time, as you'll see.

In a subsequent lesson, following the sequence described in Table 4, with the right class you could return to this sequence or a very similar one, quickly recapping some of the work above, before adding an extra level of challenge. This might involve retelling the story in the first person plural or third singular. After more consolidation work on the past tense, perhaps involving some drilling, analysis or game-like work (e.g. a Battleships game (see Chapter 6) or online conjugation game to practise verb forms), you could return to the theme of describing a journey by getting students to write their own account, either real or made up. Stress the need to reuse many of the verbs you've already practised and provide any scaffolding of the task as necessary. With the best classes this would be none at all; with the weakest this would require a gapped template. If you feel your class has difficulty processing what the pictures mean at any point, you could even run through them in English before you go into the TL. Do whatever it takes to make sure meanings are clear.

You could easily move on to some translation work, in both directions, especially if this skill is useful for the examination syllabus you're following. To recycle this type of work at a later stage you could describe another holiday you've had while students take notes in English or the TL.

Exploiting a single picture

A simple picture can be the stimulus for considerable discussion with **advanced level** students. This is extremely easy to prepare and a fun idea for creating conversation lessons. Display a simple picture featuring one or more people and use it as the basis for some **imaginative storytelling**. Here's an example with suggested questions – once again, they're written in English so you could adapt them for any language. See Figure 2.2.

Figure 2.2 Two adults talking

- *What's her name? What's his name?*

- *Where are they? What country? What town?*

- *What's their relationship? Did they meet recently? Are they work colleagues?*

- *How old are they? What are they eating? What are they talking about?*

- *What's she like as a person? What's he like? What are their interests?*

- *Why do they look so happy? How did they meet? When? Long ago?*

- *If they're married, have they been married before?*

- *What were they doing before they met at the restaurant? What are they going to do next?*

- *What do they do for a living? What do they think of their jobs?*

- *Have they always done that? What did they used to do?*

- *Do they have any guilty secrets from their past?*

- *Have they been on holiday together? Where? When?*

How the conversation develops depends on the inventiveness of your students. Tell them at the outset to be as daring as possible. They may take you in some interesting directions; or you may need to prompt them to use their imaginations a bit more by suggesting some more outrageous ideas, e.g. *he has two wives, she is a spy, he is an ex-convict, they are having an extra-marital affair* and so on.

I would do this as a teacher-led task, but with some classes you could hand out a list of suggested questions and get students to work in pairs or small groups. This would lead to a variety of stories which can be compared later on.

When you do this type of activity students come up with different scenarios. This can generate further debate. If you're leading the lesson, take them along what seems like the most fruitful linguistic and creative path. You'll find echoes of this approach in Chapter 14 where I describe TPRS (Teaching Proficiency through Reading and Storytelling) lessons.

With this task it's easy to encourage the use of different time frames – past, present and future – and to go from speaking to writing or more listening. For example, you could make up your own back-story for the couple, describe it in TL to the class, while they take notes and then summarise the account to a partner or the whole class. Or how about getting students to write an imagined dialogue between the couple once their story is established? Or ask students to find their own picture and build an imaginative story around it, either spoken, written or both. All in all, you can end up with a low-preparation lesson which generates a great deal of spontaneous TL input and output along with some creative fun. It's the kind of lesson you can do at any time, maybe as a change from your usual topics or grammar points.

Other useful pictures for this type of creative oral work might be a crime scene or a picture of a person with a headline such as "X sent to prison for 5 years" – the students would explore the person's background and the crime they may have committed.

Box 2.1: Tech tips

Easel.ly is an app with which you can reproduce infographics. It could be used by the teacher, for example, to display facts and data on a topic as a basis for discussion. Alternatively, advanced students could use it to create an infographic based on a factual text they had read.

There are many apps that allow you to add words to photos you may want to use in slides, such as **Wordswag**, **Adobe Post** and **Typorama**. You could get your lesson started with a quotation, fact or provocative statement, using a photo to support it.

Animoto produces video presentations based on photos, music and videos. You could produce attractive sets of slides with music as a basis for a storytelling activity, rather than using PowerPoint. Students could combine photos with written descriptions and sync them with Facebook.

A Tantôt is an excellent low-cost commercial website designed specifically for instant projection on to a screen. The bold, attractive visuals can be used to develop both lexical and grammatical skill. French, German, Spanish, Italian and Chinese are all covered.

Screenhunter is a basic screen capture tool if you wish to exploit screen shots. With **Screenpresso** you can edit and highlight your screenshots with a built-in image editor.

Pixabay is a source of photo images which can be used for any purpose, including commercial.

picto.qc.ca is a free bank of simple illustrations.

hcmc.uvic.ca/clipart is a bank of free clipart designed for language teachers.

Visuals for Foreign Language Instruction is a huge archive of simple black and white drawn images. It can be found here: digital.library.pitt.edu

Concluding remarks

For most people sight is the dominant sense. Pictures are undoubtedly an aid to memory, hold the attention and help make lessons more interesting: the more colourful and appealing the visuals are, the better. Don't forget you can produce your own simple pictures too – stick-characters are easy to draw. If you're not a very good artist they may be funny and engaging for students. Pictures need to be visible to every student and as unambiguous as possible. If you don't have access to technology, you can cut out pictures from magazines and blu-tack them to the board where they can be moved around. We've seen that using pictures means you can teach without using much English, which demonstrates they're an integral part of a TL approach. This isn't to say that using visuals will significantly reduce the important role of the written word. They can easily be combined with written TL forms and are just one part of a sequence of lessons involving a whole range of other activities.

CHAPTER 3

Dissecting a lesson: using written texts

Introduction

In this chapter I'm going to examine in some detail how you can work with texts. We'll look at three texts, one for **near-beginners**, one for **intermediates** and one for **advanced-level** students. Again, English text examples are used. Of course for many language teachers the written text is the go-to source for intensive input-output work. Texts may be authentic, i.e. written for native speaker readers, but are usually better when they're adapted to suit the level of the class. You want a text which is inherently interesting, ideally (but not necessarily) linked to your syllabus, possibly related to the personal lives of the students and either at their current level or just beyond it. For example, there shouldn't be too many new words or grammatical structures in a written text that you exploit in class.

Beginner level

In Box 3.1 is a short text you can use with students who've been learning the language for a few months. The rationale for this text is its inherent interest to students, the opportunities it provides for useful vocabulary and its lack of syntactic complexity. Repetition within the text makes it more teachable and there are some cognates to aid comprehension (although these will vary according to the language you're teaching). You can easily translate it for your own use.

Box 3.1: Some characters from Peppa Pig

Peppa Pig is the main character of the TV series. She's a pig. She lives in a little house with her brother George and her parents. She is the daughter in the family. She has lots of friends. She wears a red dress and black shoes. She is 7 years old and loves jumping in puddles.

Daddy Pig is Peppa's father. He is happy and likes to play with Peppa and George. He loves cookies and chocolate cake. He likes to dance and play the accordion, but he doesn't like physical exercise. He works in an office.

Mummy Pig is Peppa and George's mother. She has two children. She wears an orange dress and she sometimes wears an orange hat. She likes to do exercise in front of the television. Her favourite programme is "Mr Potato's Fitness Show".

George Pig is Peppa's little brother and Daddy Pig's son. He is 4 years old. He loves to play with his big sister. He also loves to play with his dinosaur. His dinosaur is called Mr Dinosaur.

Susan "Suzy" Sheep is Peppa's best friend. She is smart and has an excellent vocabulary. She likes to eat a lot too, for example Fruti Candy, "cheesy weenies", ice cream and pizza. She dresses like a nurse.

Possible teaching sequence

Pre-reading activities

In many cases, especially at novice level, you would prepare students for the reading of a text by pre-teaching some of the key words (in this case family vocabulary). So, let's assume you've already introduced and practised words like *parents, mother, father, son, brother, sister, daughter* and *children*. In addition students would already know words and expressions such as *he's called, she lives, house, she likes, he loves, he is X years old, she is, she has*.

New words in our text might include *pig, character, dress, shoes, jumping, puddles, happy, cookies, chocolate cake, dance, accordion, works, office, hat, programme, dinosaur, smart, vocabulary, ice cream, pizza* and *nurse*.

Now that's a fairly long list, but some of these will be cognates, e.g. in French the meaning of the following words would be obvious: *happy, cookies, chocolate cake, dance, accordion, dinosaur, smart, excellent, vocabulary* and *pizza*. So that leaves you with a suitable number of brand new words which could be dealt with in various ways. You'd leave "cheesy weenies" in the TL which will be a source of amusement as well as an example of how other languages borrow from English.

Beyond the purely linguistic pre-reading tasks, you could set up the reading in this case with a simple "We're going to learn how to talk about families. By the end of the lesson you'll know how to say something about your parents, brothers, sisters or friends. Here's a family you might know." That's all you need. Table 3.1 describes how you could go about exploiting this text.

The sequence described in Table 3.1 might take around 20–25 minutes, depending on how fast you can go with your class and how well practised they are with your techniques.

Other tasks you might do as a follow up include:

- *How do you say... in (French/German/Spanish)?*

- *How do you say ... in English?*

- *Which character am I describing?*

- (In English) "I'm now going to hide the text and read it to you again. Can you supply the next word or words when I make pauses?" (You can tailor this to the level of your class.)

- Give TL starts of sentences for students to complete orally or in writing, e.g. *Peppa lives... Daddy Pig doesn't like...* (You can leave the text displayed for this or hide it, depending on the class.)

- With the text visible give false sentences and ask students to write down the corrected answer.

- Read out multiple-choice TL statements – a, b and c. Students have to write down a, b or c. These are easy to make up on the spot, although novice teachers may like to have them all written down. Check answers with hands up or by having them write their letters on mini-whiteboards.

As in the previous chapter, the aim here has been to work in the TL nearly all the time, providing meaningful input and the chance to speak a good deal, either individually or chorally. With effective delivery and provided student behaviour is sound, this type of sequence can go quickly and enjoyably.

The next step would be to do further activities to reinforce the work in the following lesson. You could get students to change the point of view, e.g. by having Peppa describe her own family. You could then display your own family tree on the board, describe your family and do a range of interactional tasks – questioning,

Table 3.1 Exploiting a near-beginner text

Teacher	Students	Commentary
Read the whole text aloud, clearly and slowly. The text can be displayed as well as handed out.	Get the class to follow along using their fingers or by moving down a ruler as each line is complete.	This helps hold their attention. Glance around to check everyone is paying attention. Stop if this is not the case. Insist on silence of course. With some classes you might like to provide a parallel version of the text in English.
Read again, a few words at a time.	Choral repetition.	Insist on good pronunciation. Have fun with sounds.
Ask for volunteers to read a paragraph each.	Hands up. Volunteers read aloud.	Check the rest of the class are listening. At this level, reading aloud short sections is best. Let the most confident students show off. Use gentle correction.
Get students to read in pairs.	Students read to each other.	Check all students are on task.
Whole-class true/false statements, e.g. Peppa is a dinosaur, Peppa is 8 years old, George is the son, Daddy likes exercise, etc.	Hands up. Individual answers true/false.	Do this at pace, making up silly or outrageous false statements with cognates, e.g. George is a dinosaur, Peppa is a giraffe. Humour helps. Young students like absurdity, so attention is maintained and you get to recycle lots of language.
Now just give false statements and tell students they have to correct them.	Hands up and no hands up. Individual answers, some group repetition.	Now the students have to do more work by combining comprehension with more production (input-output). Get students to repeat chorally. Keep up the pace.
Now, the next step up: ask questions in TL about the text. Tell the students you'll use the word who (translate it for clarity – it's really important). *Who is Peppa?* *Does Peppa live in a big house?* etc.	Hands up and no hands up. Individual answers. Some choral repetition.	You can always grab students' attention by saying "Now this bit's really important. I'd like you to listen extra hard." Use the full range of question types: yes/no, either/or, question-word questions, e.g. How old is she/ Where does she live? (Students may need prompting about question words.)
Ask the class if they have any questions.	Hands up.	For vocabulary use gesture, synonyms or translation.
Distribute a handout with a gapped transcription of the text. Supply missing words out of order at the bottom.	Students work in silence.	By now the class, if they've managed to keep going, will have heard the language items multiple times, so a transition is probably needed.

true/false and so on. You could have students do a survey around the class to find out the "average family", then compare it with some official statistics for general interest. The final goal of all these tasks might be to get students to write or record (even memorise) descriptions of their own family either in the third or first person.

Intermediate level

With intermediate students you clearly have access to a wider range of texts. If the class isn't the quickest you can work on relatively complex and interesting texts using the parallel text approach (the TL text on the left of the page, the English translation on the right). All groups, whatever their aptitude or attainment, can benefit from parallel text work. However, I'm now going to describe a sequence based on a typical intermediate text, chosen for its general interest and appropriate difficulty level. The text is in Box 3.2.

Box 3.2: Interview with Karen, an astronaut

1   **How long have you worked for NASA?**
    I've been at NASA for 13 years. I'm employed by the American government.

2   **What training do you need to do to become an astronaut?**
    Of course, to be considered as an astronaut you have to be good at maths and science, but you also need a good all-round education to be able to communicate with engineers and scientists. You also have to speak other languages because we work with astronauts from around the world, especially Russia and Europe.

3   **What kind of physical requirements are needed to become an astronaut?**
    You can't be too tall or too short! Apart from that you have to be in good general health and not suffer from any illness that cannot be treated in space.

4   **How did you become an astronaut?**
    Mainly I was lucky! When I left secondary school I went to the US naval Academy and went into naval aviation. I flew with an oceanographic research team doing research and collecting data about the oceans. I then left the navy and went to work as an engineer at the Kennedy Space Centre in Florida. I worked on rocket mechanical systems before being chosen as an astronaut.

5   **How many times have you been into space?**
    I've done just one visit to the International Space Station. I stayed there for three months.

---

6   **What were your responsibilities?**
I was a mission specialist. We supervised 25 different experiments and I assisted the mission leader with the experiments.

7   **What were your daily responsibilities on the ground?**
One of the main things we do is continue our training for the day we go into space.

8   **What's your favourite aspect of the work?**
Working as a team. There are seven members in a crew. We train together for years and you develop a great friendship with your team.

Possible teaching sequence

Note how each task below builds up the level of challenge and takes the class with you step by step.

1. Pre-reading task

Show a three minute extract from a video about the International Space Station. These are easy to find on YouTube. Here's a fun example available in 2017 which shows a female astronaut washing her hair in space:

www.youtube.com/watch?v=uIjNfZbUYu8

The point to make here is that some classes will happily dive straight into a text-based lesson with minimal preparation, but others need to be gently led into the water and have their interest aroused before starting the "real work". This is an example of sweetening the pill, if you will. The three minutes spent watching and listening in English are time well spent if the pay-off is greater commitment to the task later.

2. Pre-teach some vocabulary

Don't hand out or display the text immediately. Display some key TL words that relate to the theme of the text:

space   engineering   rocket   scientist   health
aviation   mission   experiment

Do a *How do you say in French/German/Spanish* task. Then say, in TL or English, depending on the class, that they're going to read an interview with someone. Can they guess who it might be?

3. Hand out the text

It's worth noting here the difference between displaying a text on screen and handing it out. If you display a text it forces students to look up and towards you and the board as you're working. You can point to or highlight aspects of the text and use your interactive whiteboard to do other things such as take out certain words, blur sections or highlight words and chunks in colour. On the other hand, if students have a text on their tables they can mark it in various ways and have it to keep. There's clearly merit in taking advantage of both means.

4. Read the text aloud

With an excellent class you could have a student read the questions while you read the answers. This would add an extra level of interest for the other students. My experience is that reading aloud is better than having students read silently since the latter approach leads some students to switch off. In any case, they need to hear you read as a good model so they can link the sounds with the words. Remember that research clearly shows the sound of a word plays a vital role in helping students remember it.

5. Get students to read aloud

This allows for a second pass at the text. Depending on the class, get individual students to read aloud short extracts, either asking for volunteers or choosing students you wish to show their skills. Involve as many students as possible and don't worry about reading the same section more than once. Do some gentle correction as required. Students can then read to each other in pairs, after which you can ask them to say which words they found difficult.

6. True/false questioning

Make about ten true/false statements in TL about the text. Students raise their hands and offer answers. You can correct the false statements yourself, providing extra input in the process. With weaker classes you might do this in English. You could then get the class to do it in pairs. Remember that intermediate classes are less keen on playing the teacher-led question-answer game than younger groups, so moving to pair work is often a good strategy if the mood and behaviour are right. Give them a time limit: "You have three minutes to make up some true/false statements for your partner."

7. Make false statements

Give about ten false statements for students to correct. Students put up their hands to correct, supplying more of their own input this time. Your statements can be as subtle or absurd as you want.

8. Ask questions in TL

Follow the same sequence as the text and vary the difficulty level of the questions, making sure you include some really easy ones. This is an example of using differentiated questioning in the classroom. You can use no hands up for the easier questions to make sure that the whole class is paying attention.

- *What's her name?*

- *Who does she work for?*

- *Has she worked there for 50 years?* (This question supplies some content students can use in the answer – "she has worked there".)

- *How long has she worked there?* (This question is harder since part of the answer is not supplied in your question.)

- *Which subjects are important for being an astronaut?*

- *What subjects do you prefer?* (This personalises the topic and allows you to recycle previously learned language about school subjects.)

And so on.
    You might like to finish with *Would you like to be an astronaut? Why? Why not?*

9. Complete a gapped version of the text

This would be a reading/writing task and you can make it as easy or hard as you want, depending on the class. With a very low-attaining class you could even do it in English. You could supply a set of words for students to pick from. You can include irrelevant words to make the task a little more challenging or even amusing.

10. Extension task: recreate the interview

With a high-attaining class you could then hide the text, or just leave some brief notes displayed on the board and get the class into pairs to play journalist and astronaut, improvising the dialogue. You can even suggest that students make up other invented details which didn't appear in the written text.

11. Writing/homework task

Students write a TL report of about 120 words in the third person about the astronaut. With some classes you might supply a template or gapped version of the task. In any case, the task needs to be finely tuned to the class's abilities, not too easy, not too hard. In a mixed ability class you could offer a template for some students, but not others. (I would be hesitant about this, however, because of the inherent labelling of students involved with this approach.)

The point of this section has been to demonstrate that a text at intermediate level can be a source of "multi-modal" activities, i.e. involving listening, speaking, reading and writing, with each skill reinforcing the others as well as students' overall command of the language. In general, if the homework culture is good at your school, I'd try to make writing the main element of homework, maximising class time for other skills. The timetabling arrangements in your school might make this hard to achieve, however. If you have a two-hour lesson to fill, for example, writing will inevitably form part of the lesson plan. For a lengthy list of the many types of interaction you can use when working with texts, see Chapter 12.

Advanced level

It's at this level that you can extract the utmost from interesting written texts. Students are at a standard where they can access a good deal more content while the sources of texts are wide ranging. Choice of text remains critical. If you're following a specified syllabus you'll be strongly guided by this, but don't let this stop you going *off piste* by using random texts that are just really interesting or, for example, relevant to recent news events. Part of being an effective teacher is feeling independent enough to trust your own judgement regarding which texts motivate students.

The received wisdom is that texts ought to relate to students' own interests as far as possible. I'd add that great language educators also value the importance of opening students' minds to new information and ideas. In a sense, teaching a language at advanced level is partly about doing "general studies in another language". In other words, you can and should create new interests for students, not just take advantage of existing ones. The language can now become just a natural means of exchanging interesting ideas.

Furthermore, at advanced level, when you probably have more time per week with the class and students have more time for independent study, you can really exploit the natural dimension of second language learning. As you may know, some scholars (most famously Stephen Krashen) argue that acquiring a second language is essentially the same as acquiring one's first language and that, therefore, all you need to make it happen is to supply meaningful messages. But for this to be effective, you need to supply lots of comprehensible input. At advanced level you have a much greater chance of achieving this aim. Texts are an excellent medium for supplying masses of input which can then be exploited with further input-output activities.

In Box 3.3 is the text we'll use for the next teaching sequence. It's about living on the streets in Berlin. Once again, you could easily translate it into the language you teach.

Box 3.3: Birgit's story

At 2 years old, Birgit was placed in a foster home because her mother was unable to care for her. She grew up in the countryside in what she thought was a strange and hostile world. At 17 years, she decided to run away and found herself in Berlin – without anything or anyone. She became a woman living on the street. Poverty, beatings, alcohol, she experienced it all. Here is what she said:

"When I left my foster family at 17, I decided to take refuge in friends' places in Berlin. One evening I found myself in an eastern suburb. Some friends refused to put me up, others just didn't respond. I wandered the streets trying to enter buildings until a door finally opened. I entered, lay down in a hallway and tried to sleep through the night, but it was impossible. In the street, most of the time, the homeless spend the night walking around. They prefer to sleep during the day when there are people around; it's safer."

"The worst part was the rain. You have to live outdoors to realise how bad it is. You end up smelling like a wet dog, which is disgusting for other people. To avoid this, you take refuge in doorways, bars, but end up being moved on. People call the cops to get rid of us."

"There are far fewer women than men in the street. It's much more dangerous for a woman to be on the streets. Women often look for men who, for various reasons, open their doors. Then some women decide to have a child; it's a good way to get support from social services. Either you have relationships with men who protect you, or you must be cunning. Many times I have done anything to get a bed in hospital. Some of my homeless friends have even got themselves sent to prison just to be warm and to get enough to eat."

"I always had the idea that one day I would get a home – and I didn't even look like a homeless person. I always wore make-up, even if it meant stealing someone else's. I often went into railway stations to wash. In one station I got to know the lady who cleaned the toilets. We often talked together, I took the opportunity to do my make-up and change clothes in the bathroom."

"Then I met Claudia, a journalist, who has changed my life. In 2016, I was offered a small room on the top floor of her block. In exchange, I had to take care of her children and pet cat. Today, I sometimes see my friends in the street. I help them as much as I can, although many older friends have died. We have a drink together; I give them cigarettes. Sometimes they call me and I help them to find a pair of shoes or a shirt. They really appreciate having someone speak on their behalf."

Possible teaching sequence

1. Pre-reading

Display some words on the board:

streets   drugs   sleep   pavement   doorway   poverty   begging

Then ask questions in TL:

• *What do you think this text will be about?*

Then:

• *What's a homeless person?*

- *Why do people become homeless?*

- *Where do you find most homeless people?*

- *What help is offered to people living on the streets?*

- *How do homeless people survive?*

2. Read aloud the text

Even at advanced level I'd read aloud a text in order that students have an opportunity to follow the language at a steady pace, hearing the words pronounced. Your own stress and intonation also assist in establishing meaning.

3. Questions in TL

- *Who is Birgit?*

- *Why was she placed in a foster home?*

- *How old was she then?*

- *What did she think of the world she grew up in?*

- *What happened when she was 17?*

- *Why did she choose to go to Berlin? (and so on)*

4. Pair-work questions

Provide a list of written questions similar or identical to the ones you've just asked. Students take turns at asking each other these questions. This allows students to recycle the language for themselves. Weaker students will gain confidence from this. You can take a well-earned breather and monitor from a distance.

5. Focus on vocabulary

Seek definitions of words in the text. This makes students reread and allows them an opportunity to produce original utterances based on their prior knowledge.

- *What's a foster home?*

- *What's the opposite of poverty?*

- *What's a suburb? What's the opposite of suburb?*

- *What's the opposite of outdoors?*

- *What do social services do?*

- *Find the word which means something you put on your face to look prettier.*

- *Find the word for the place you go when you've committed a crime.*

Note that questions like this may seem artificial, but they're designed to provide more TL input as well as focus on vocabulary building. You can adapt their level to your class.

6. Paired creative speaking

By now the students should know the text and language well enough to do a more unstructured fluency task. For example:

- *In pairs imagine one of you is a journalist and the other is Birgit. Recreate the interview.*

- *In pairs, one of you tries to talk as long as possible about Birgit's story while the other notes down any language errors they detect.*

7. Provide written exercises based on the text

These can include, for example, a bilingual vocabulary list to complete, true/false/not mentioned statements, TL questions, matching starts and ends of sentences while hiding the text and translation in both directions. These may be best done as independent work.

It's easy to see how a text of this type might form part of a broader unit of work on poverty, to include audio and video listening (see Chapter 5), a "web quest" reading task based on a charity web site and a chosen area of grammar to work on. It's worth noting in passing that, at advanced level, you're rarely going to use a text with the main aim of drilling a particular grammatical structure, but the use of a structure in a text could form the basis of some grammar-focused practice. Our example text might lend itself to the practice of object pronouns, for example.

> ### Box 3.4: Tech tips
>
> The **interactive whiteboard** can come into its own when working with texts. Various tools can be used to vary the display of texts, colour code words or phrases, highlight grammatical features, hide words and chunks and so on. Use the curtain tool to reveal text line by line.
>
> **Textivate** allows you to display texts and do language manipulation tasks. More commonly, though, it is used by students working individually with a tablet or computer. Textivate is a way for teachers to create multiple interactive exercises and worksheets based on texts, which can then be used in many different ways, shared by other teachers and accessed by students. Activity types include: text-building, jigsaw reading, gap-filling, matching and anagrams.
>
> **Languages Online** is a source of texts accompanied by Hot Potato text manipulation and drag-and-drop tasks.
>
> **Boardworks** contains examples of texts with accompanying interactive whiteboard activities. Course book packages usually include text-based computer and tablet materials.

Concluding remarks

Authentic or not?

Some teachers place a high value on the use of authentic reading resources, but I'd argue for adapted authentic texts in most cases, even at advanced level. More important than authenticity is the level of difficulty and interest. An authentic text can be dull and too hard; an adapted text can be interesting and at the right level. I'd choose the latter.

Intensive practice

A recurring point in this chapter has been my preference for working on a text intensively, providing plenty of input and opportunities for practice. That's not to downplay the value of reading extensively or for general interest, but it's my view that outstanding teachers make maximum use of a text in class, working at pace, allowing students time to take in meaning and practise the language in stimulating ways, both controlled and less structured. Students gain a greater feeling of mastery in this fashion.

Explain what you're doing

It does no harm at all to let students in to your secret about how languages are acquired. Why not explain a little to them about how skills are developed through practice and how young children acquire their first language? This may help to get students go along with your approach and motivate them just a little more to work independently.

CHAPTER 4

Dissecting a lesson: task-based lessons

Introduction

This chapter will focus on managing effective and stimulating task-based lessons for students of all levels. I'll present a rationale for making occasional use of a task-based approach, then follow with a few examples of effective lessons. The main points will be to show how effective teachers recognise the value of using language for a practical purpose, the importance of the communicative principle known as the **information gap** and the need to allow students an opportunity to use the language independently. I'll again emphasise how important it is to provide stimulating, cognitively challenging comprehensible input to allow the natural processes of language acquisition to occur.

Rationale

Teachers are often concerned by the fact that classroom language learning is an artificial process with which many students find it hard to engage. The link between learning vocabulary, studying topics, practising verb forms, and the real world of speaking a language seems tenuous. Many students are happy to go along with the process, motivated by pleasing the teacher, getting grades or passing an exam for their future study or career. Some have travelled, already speak a second language or are part of motivated families who value language learning and engaging with other cultures. But we have to acknowledge that many students take some convincing that learning a language is worthwhile.

With this in mind, some see **content-based** (sometimes called CLIL – Content and Language Integrated Learning) and **task-based** approaches as a partial solution. These place an equally high or even higher value on the content or task as on the language itself. This, so some teachers find, makes the work more motivating. The argument goes that students are not likely to find talking about what's in their pencil case or conjugating the verb *to be* inherently stimulating or even cognitively challenging. They might, however, find the following types of activity of greater interest:

- online shopping;

- working on a problem-solving task;

- doing a project with a partner class;

- producing a class newspaper or web magazine;

- creating a menu for a restaurant;

- making a recipe following a TL menu;

- learning another subject through the medium of the TL;

- solving a murder mystery.

Let's look at how we might exploit some of these examples.

Online shopping

This is a very easy task to organise and one which students can enjoy at various levels. I'm going to give an example for **near-beginners**, based on **buying food online**.

Produce a shopping list of items in English for the students to buy from a suitable online store which is easy to navigate and contains clear pictures and prices. Make sure you've checked the site to be sure all items are available. Explain to the class that their job is to browse the site and fill their trolley at the lowest price possible. Students of this age will not have bought groceries online, so there's a real-life skill to be acquired here too. As they work (largely in silence), your job is to monitor that they are all on the right site, answer occasional questions and assist with any navigation problems. If any students finish early you can provide some extra items to search or just let them browse. This task works well with other shopping items, notably clothing and household goods.

Table 4.1 shows an example grid I've used in French lessons with students in their second year of learning. The supermarket site was *auchan.fr*. You can create a spreadsheet file which will even calculate the total price for the students.

Table 4.1 Online shopping list

Anglais	Français	Quantité	Prix
Apples (Golden)		1kg	
Pears		500g	
Bananas		500g	
Kiwis		500g	
Pineapple		1	
Tomatoes		500g	
Potatoes		1kg	
Cabbage (green)		1	
Cauliflower		1	
Courgettes		500g	
Onions		500g	
Garlic		1 packet	
Beef (sirloin)		1kg	
Chicken		1	
Lamb (chops)		1	
Jam (Bonne Maman)		2	
Tin of apricots		1	
Ketchup		1	
Green olives (whole)		1 pot	
Olive oil (own brand)		1 litre	
Eggs		6	
Butter (salted)		250g	
Milk (semi-skimmed)		2 litres	
Camembert		1	
Yogurt (with fruit bits)		16	
Pâté		1	
Croissants		10 x 40g	
Cider (cheapest)		1 litre	
Water (Perrier)		1 litre	
Cornflakes		500g	
Potato crisps		6	

A task such as this could be set at the end of a teaching sequence about food and quantities, or even used as an introduction to the topic. It allows students to browse the site, copy down correct spellings on the grid and, in the process, learn how to get best value! It's an excellent way to spend about 45 minutes in a computer room, or to use tablets in class.

Producing a class newspaper or webzine

To set up this project with an **intermediate** class, produce a list of features you want to see in your paper or on your site, e.g. news stories, a weather report, an astrology page, advertisements, sports stories, a star interview and crossword. The class is divided into small teams whose job it is to produce material from one of these categories. You could assign relatively harder tasks to some groups. It's important to model at least some of the items, giving them access, say, to a booklet showing similar material. Text books often supply useful models.

If you adopt an old-school approach you could literally cut and paste the material which the students produce into a printed newspaper which can be read by the whole class. It's more likely, however, that you'd do the task digitally, sharing files via a VLE (Virtual Learning Environment) or other sharing platform such as Google Classroom, Google Drive or Dropbox. The material could be merged to produce an online paper or set of web pages readable by the class or even other students in the school.

The principal challenge with this type of task is to ensure students work efficiently, therefore they require a strict deadline. If you think this sort of work is beyond your students you could scaffold the task by supplying part-finished pieces for them to work on. Typically you'd allocate about three hours to the whole project, some of which could be homework. The linguistic benefits are clear: reading and practice at compositional writing involving translation and dictionary use.

Making a recipe

For this activity for **intermediate** students you need a simple TL recipe that requires the ingredients students' families are likely to have at home. Ideally the recipe would be a common one associated with the TL culture. For French classes I've used two recipes, one for almond biscuits and one for an onion tart.

Instruct the students to read the recipe, translate it into English (to show evidence they've used the TL recipe, not another one), then make it, possibly with the aid of their parents. If you think any children don't have access to what they need at home, you could enlist the help of the food technology department in your school where the class could make the recipe. Once the recipe is complete you can have a tasting in class. This could become the basis of a further linguistic task (describing food).

One point to make here is that, even if the linguistic or cultural returns on a task are not so great, there's room for the occasional really memorable activity which provides students with a positive association with your subject. There aren't that many lessons students later recall by saying "Do you remember when...?"

Producing a video news bulletin

This project would suit **advanced-level** students in groups of about four and involves team working, reading, TL discussion and presenting. This is the task:

> You and your group are on the editorial team whose job is to produce this evening's TV news bulletin. You have a list of news stories which have come in to your office. Discuss their relative merits, choose six and put them in order based on importance. You then need to write a script, choose a news anchor or two and reporters. Scripts need to be written, a teleprompt produced, then the bulletin filmed on video to be shown to the rest of the class. You have two lessons of two hours to complete the task.

Box 4.1: List of news stories

1 *The unemployment rate has risen this month to 5.6 per cent. There are now an extra 30,000 jobseekers.*
2 *An earthquake in Turkey reaching 7.0 on the Richter scale has killed an estimated 300 people.*
3 *Following a motorway pile-up south of Leeds, five people have been killed and 15 injured.*
4 *A major road accident in Spain has killed 20 people and injured 35. The weather was foggy at the time.*
5 *Germany beat Spain 2–0 in the semi-final of the European Championships.*
6 *Astronomers say they have detected a new planet at the edge of our solar system.*
7 *A man in Texas claims that his dog can speak English. We have film.*
8 *Scientists are now predicting that global temperatures will rise by at least 3 degrees by the end of this century. The consequences could be devastating.*

9   The latest James Bond movie opens tomorrow in London with the new Bond played by Idris Elba.

10   A petroleum tanker has run aground off the coast of Brittany. Large amounts of oil are already polluting several kilometres of beach in France.

11   China announces that it will send two astronauts to the moon next year.

12   Singer Beyoncé has announced that she is retiring from recording and touring.

Running the task

1. Setting up

Explain the project. Get students into groups (you may wish to engineer this so there is a range of attainment in each group). Emphasise that the task will be conducted almost entirely in TL and it will stop if this rule is broken. Set out the time limit and the fact that any extra work will have to be done independently. Explain the different roles required in the group. They'll need a phone to film with and a teleprompt system – large rolls of paper or, if possible, a digital teleprompt system (these are easy to find online and your technically minded students will sort this out).

Note that students can get quite excited about this activity and therefore will be tempted to speak in English. You may need to stress the valuable speaking practice students get while doing the task.

2. Language preparation

Display and hand out some of the useful language the students will need to negotiate this task; Examples are in Box 4.2.

Box 4.2: News-bulletin language

In my opinion	I don't agree	Do you think that...?	On the other hand
We could...	We should...	Tonight's top stories	Let's hear from...
To be interested in	To be bored by	Of great importance	Relevant
I think that	Presenter	Reporter	Interview
On the spot	Why don't we...?	Topical	News report

---

3. Supervising the task

For a good deal of the time you can just be available for language help and to encourage everyone to take part. Quieter groups may need some extra input to get them underway. Don't worry if you have to speak quite a bit to groups as this is all useful extra TL input. When students are scripting their reports you can do some correcting to help them.

4. Presenting the task

Some students may want to dress up, film outside reports or use the whiteboard for supporting visuals. They may come up with a theme tune for their bulletin. They can do more than one take and their news bulletins can be uploaded to YouTube if they want. The process is more important than the final product.

If you have concerns that a project of this sort is time consuming and will only yield a certain amount of language practice, weigh this up once more against the fact that students find such tasks both enjoyable and memorable. Perhaps part of becoming an outstanding teacher is being willing to take a few risks and let the class do their own thing!

Murder mystery

Explain to your group of **advanced** students that the Head Teacher of a school has been murdered. Then hand out some slips of paper that contain clues to what happened. The students have to work out between themselves who perpetrated the crime, why and how. This works best when you almost completely withdraw from the task, letting students themselves work out who committed the murder. Tables 4.2 shows the clues (imagine them in TL) which you would cut out and distribute, two or three to each student depending on the size of the group. If the activity is slow to get going, suggest that one student plays the role of leader and writes up notes on the board as students read aloud from their slips.

The solution is as follows: having learned that she was about to be dismissed for her incompetence, the secretary poured some slow-acting poison into the Head Teacher's coffee. He died of a heart attack at 12.10 as a result of the poison. The PE teacher had opened a tin of red paint with the screwdriver he'd borrowed. The Head had cut his neck while shaving that morning.

Table 4.2 Cue cards for murder mystery task

Dr Jones the physics teacher thinks he's an astronaut and does "moon walks".	Mrs Jay the secretary is making more and more mistakes and is worried she will get fired.	Mr Davies the Deputy Principal is highly ambitious and would like to take over the head's job.	Miss Broom, the Spanish teacher, recently met a Colombian man who is in a drug-smuggling ring.
The Head has learned about Miss Broom's relationship and is going to report it to the police.	The Deputy Principal was in the Head's office at 11.55 for a meeting.	The Head was found murdered in his office at 12.15.	The secretary made a cup of coffee for the Head at 11.00.
The police discovered traces of a slow-acting poison in a waste paper bin in the secretary's office.	The secretary took in a cup of coffee to the Head at 11.05.	The Head was suffering from a heart condition which made him susceptible to chemical stimulants.	At 11.20 the PE teacher, Mr Casey, was seen in the gym carrying a screwdriver with something red on it.
When the Head's body was discovered his arm had a cut on it and he was bleeding slightly.	The PE teacher went to see the Head at 11.45 to tell him about the latest sports results.	The Spanish teacher learned from the geography teacher that the Head knew about her new boyfriend.	The physics teacher learned that he was soon to be fired because of his mental health problems.
When Mr Davies met the Head in his office he did not have any coffee.	The PE teacher asked to borrow a screwdriver from the technology teacher at 10.00.	At 12.05 the Head received a call from his Board of Governors telling him he would be losing his job.	Mr Casey had a conversation with Miss Broom at 11.30. He said he had just had a row with the Head about his salary.
The physics teacher had a heated conversation with the Head in his office at 11.40.	When the Head's body was found there were red marks on his neck.	Miss Broom illegally kept a small gun in her handbag for self-defence.	The Spanish teacher was asked by the secretary to go and see the Head at 12.00.
At 11.20 the Deputy Principal went to see the Head. They argued about the new uniform rules.	Mr Mackenzie, the technology teacher, gave a screwdriver to Mr Casey during break at 11.10.	Mr Mackenzie didn't get on with the Head Teacher very well, but he respected him.	The secretary opened a letter at 10.00. It was about her imminent dismissal.
Miss Broom often visited South America where she had some friends involved in drug-trafficking.	During the morning the physics teacher was seen by some students in a corridor. He was walking strangely, as if on air.	During his meeting with the Deputy Principal the Head complained of indigestion.	Miss Broom went to the secretary's office at 11.00. She left with a smile on her face.

Interview a grandparent

This task has the linguistic goal of practising use of the imperfect ("used to") tense. Having presented and thoroughly practised the imperfect tense (see Chapter 7) you can tell students as a homework task to interview a grandparent, elderly relative, or even a parent or carer. Provide them with a series of questions to ask in English: "Where did you live as a child? What music did you listen to? What did you watch on TV? What did you eat and drink? What did your parents do for a living? How was life different?" etc. They then have to write up their answers in the form of a short essay in the TL. They could also record their work digitally. With fast groups you don't need to provide any more resources, but with lower-attaining students you could provide gapped answers for them to fill in. They would have to do some dictionary work to find the TL words needed to fill the gaps. This task gets students talking with their family and I'm sure they learn a good deal in the process. You can imagine that this would be an unusually motivating homework assignment for many students.

Information gaps

At a simpler level, the information gap principle allows you to set up easy task-based activities which require students to exchange information for a purpose. For these to work you will have to provide a **need to communicate** and give each partner **information the other doesn't possess**. These can be the simplest of guessing games, requiring minimal preparation. Information gap activities are useful for various reasons. They provide an opportunity for extended speaking practice, they represent real communication, motivation can be high, and they require skills such as clarifying meaning and rephrasing. Typical information gaps include: describe and draw, spot the difference, jigsaw reading, jigsaw listening and split dictations (where each partner has a different partial transcript).

Here are five minimal preparation guessing games which exploit the information gap principle:

1. Last weekend

For **low-intermediates**. Get each partner to write down five real or invented activities they did over the previous weekend. Each partner has to guess what the other person did by asking yes/no questions. Encourage students to come up with original or wacky ideas. This is good for practising the past (preterite) tense.

2. Shopping list

For **near-beginners**. Each person writes down a list of ten items they're going to buy at the supermarket. Each partner has to guess the other's list.

3. Mute customer

Any level. Again, based on a shopping list or just a set of words. Each partner has a list and must explain what's on their list by using gesture, not words. This is fun for reviewing vocabulary at various levels.

4. Holiday plans

Intermediate. Each partner lists ten things they're going to do during the next holiday. Partners use yes/no questions to work out the other person's list. This is effective for future or immediate future tense usage.

5. Proverbs

Advanced. Display on the board in two columns a list of, say, 16 proverbs or sayings in the TL. Alternatively provide a handout with the proverbs written in two columns. Make sure students understand them, preferably by explaining in the TL. You could translate if you want to get on to the pair work quickly, but the advantage of using the TL is that students already hear a model of how to explain the sayings. Then, each partner chooses five proverbs or sayings and attempt to exemplify or explain them while the other student tries to guess what they are. Partners could prompt each other for further information. This is good for creative use of language at a higher level.

Activities such as the above can be easily tacked on to a more traditional task to spice up a lesson, give you a much-needed rest and add variety. Skilled teachers know when to stop leading from the front and when to change the perspective of a lesson, allowing students to listen a bit less and talk more.

Here are three more examples:

6. Hotel problems (intermediate)

Each partner has a role card. A solution to the problem must be found.

Student A: *You are a guest staying at a hotel. The hotel website says it is a four-star luxury hotel, but in your room the sheets and towels are dirty, the bathroom is too small, the street outside is very noisy and … (make up two more problems). You want to change to a better room and you want a reduction on your bill. Talk to the receptionist and solve the problem.*

Student B: *You are a hotel receptionist. There is a guest staying at the hotel who complains about everything, even when there isn't a problem. You are allowed to move a guest to a different room, but you cannot change the price of a room. Talk to the guest and try to resolve the issue.*

7. Where is the ghost? (near-beginners)

In this example each partner has a side-on view of a two storey house, depicting furniture and ghosts in various places. The ghosts are in different places in each partner's picture. By asking yes/no questions each partner has to find out where their partner's ghosts are. This task would fit very well at the end of a sequence about house and home.

8. Finding personal information (low-intermediate)

Table 4.3 Information gap task: finding personal information

Student card A

Name	Home town	Family	Job	Pastimes	Movies
Sophie		42, married, 2 children	doctor		romcoms
			teacher	reading (science fiction)	
Lionel	Barcelona			video games	action
			social worker	baking	
Jean-Paul	Toulouse				dramas

Dissecting a lesson: task-based lessons

Student card B

Name	Home town	Family	Job	Pastimes	Movies
	Manchester			running	
Mario	Milan	27, single			horror
		32, married with one child	journalist		
Georgia	Berlin	living with Harry			foreign
		40, married to David	IT	playing saxophone	

The aim of the task is for each student to complete their card (see Table 4.3) by asking their partner appropriate TL questions. This activity fits well later in a sequence of work about using questions. It's assumed that you've explained and practised this rigorously beforehand and that students have gained a little automaticity and know how to use the words *what, where (from), how old, what kind, who with* along with the appropriate question syntax for the language concerned. Before starting the task, rehearse with the class on the board how to ask the questions they need. With some classes you may need to leave these questions displayed, or at least a gapped version of them. Alternatively, you could leave them visible, then gradually erase parts during the activity, depending on how well students are getting on. Following are the questions they need.

- *What is the first person's name? How do you spell it?*

- *Where's he/she from?*

- *How old is he/she? What is their family situation?*

- *What does he/she do for a living?*

- *What does he/she like doing in their spare time?*

- *What kind of movies does he/she like?*

You may prefer to explain the task in English. If this gets students underway quickly and confidently it's worth the time saved. Clarity of instructions is so important when setting up a task. With higher-attaining groups you could get students to volunteer more information than is given on the cards, giving them some scope for creativity and humour.

Once the pairs are working you can take a back seat, checking that the task is proceeding in the TL. You need to be available for questions or to help along any pairs having difficulty. To bring the activity to a close you can ask individuals to summarise what they know about each person, thus putting at least six sentences together in a row.

The value of this activity lies in the repetition required, the opportunity to listen and speak under little pressure from the teacher and the fact that there is a clear task to be completed. One issue that arises when running tasks like this is that some pairs will finish more quickly than others. In this case, have a second pair of cards available.

Box 4.3: Tech tips

As usual, look for tasks rich in TL input. Avoid tasks where too much time is spent on creation and too little on language learning activity.

Plan a holiday for a family

Use review websites such as **Booking.com or TripAdvisor**. They would need to include at least five different destinations, summarising each one in writing either in English or the TL. The same can be done for sites featuring **holiday homes** and **campsites**.

Plan a visit to a theme park

Using a TL website, plan a day's visit incorporating which rides you'll do, where you'll eat, how you'll get there, when you'll arrive and leave. This would naturally be a good fit for using the future tense.

Support a charity

Advanced students can be given four different TL charity websites to study, together with a set of questions to research, e.g. What does the charity support? How does

---

it raise funds? What is its history? etc. The task is, with reading and note-taking, to choose a charity to support and justify the decision.

Share work online

As mentioned earlier, some teachers find **Google Classroom**, **Google Drive** or **Dropbox** an effective and convenient way for students to share their work for reading and assessment by the teacher. Others use a school-based **VLE** (Virtual Learning Environment), e.g. **Moodle**, for the same purpose.

Teleprompter apps and websites are numerous. There are free ones, including for tablets, or more sophisticated premium versions.

Concluding remarks

Project and task-based approaches have advantages but they also have their limitations. Why? Although they may be motivating for students because of their content or inherent interest as a task, it's hard to make them fit within a structured curriculum based on progressing from easy to harder language. Texts you want to use for some projects can be too difficult and students may lack the skills to communicate as well as they'd like. It generally makes most sense to make occasional use of tasks or bigger projects to supplement your normal scheme of work or curriculum plan. If you can make them fit within your topic curriculum, even better. You might also like the idea of doing them with classes as an end of term special activity when you're running out of steam and want students to be working independently.

When you do a task or content-based project of any sort, you need to decide to what extent you focus purely on the content or the language to be used. If you end up doing lots of language exercises, you may remove some of the interest from the topic itself. So there's a balance to be struck. This approach may also suit teachers who prefer to encourage a greater degree of group work and learner autonomy. If your school's culture leans towards this end of the spectrum, content- and task-based approaches may be a decent fit. Overall, however, although they may offer advantages in terms of motivation and add variety, if used on their own they are unlikely to lead to higher attainment in the long run.

Chapter 5

Enjoying sounds

Introduction

In this chapter the focus is on listening, the most important, yet often neglected skill. How do skilled teachers develop confident listeners? I'm going to look at a range of phonological tasks that enable beginners to enjoy hearing and using unfamiliar sounds. I'll emphasise the importance of linking sound to spelling to reinforce memory links (phonics) and examine what it means to **teach** listening, rather than just test it. Listening tests are often the ones students fear most (over in a short time, with no time to reflect and review). I'll offer examples of specific tasks, including using online video, transcribing tasks, gap-fill, matching tasks and multi-skill tasks featuring a strong listening element. I'll also show how you can improve students' grammar through listening and pose some provocative questions about how you might be teaching listening now.

Phonics fun

How do we get youngsters to enjoy strange sounds? How do we get them to pronounce well? How do we take the fear out of listening?

From the very beginning it's important to be demanding with your expectations about pronunciation. If your students develop good pronunciation habits in their first year, this will continue into the future. If you make do with second-class pronunciation, students will rarely develop the right habits. What's more, if students try hard and are fussy about sounding like a native speaker, they'll become more discerning listeners in turn. Research suggests that having a good phonological memory assists with word retention in general. Fortunately, most students enjoy playing with new sounds if you create the right conditions. Below are some tips of the trade.

Enjoying sounds

- Drill isolated sounds, linking them to spelling, e.g. in French use the phrase *un bon vin blanc* to practise the four nasal vowels; explain how you make a French *u* or German *ü* sound by trying to say *ee* while rounding your lips; explain the mechanics of making a uvular *r* sound in French and German, or a rolled *r* in Spanish.

- Show students a side-on diagram of the mouth with the main articulators and how they work to create specific sounds (see Figure 5.1). Give them some basic phonetics terminology to get them interested in the science of sounds, e.g. the terms plosive, voicing, fricative, bilabial, uvula, dental, alveolar and palatal.

- When doing choral repetition exaggerate sounds a little and encourage students to do the same; show them clear mouth shapes.

- Group words together with the same vowel sounds, e.g. when displaying words on PowerPoint slides for repetition work. Point out how different letter combinations can produce the same sound (notably in French).

- Be acutely aware of the sounds which will cause difficulty for English native speakers, e.g. all French vowels, *r* sounds in all languages, German fricatives (*ch*) and diphthongs, Spanish bilabial, sibilant (*s*) and fricative (*j*) sounds. Focus on them and have fun making them.

- Link gestures to sounds and spellings, e.g. raising your arms or fingers for certain accents or diacritics.

- Use tongue twisters.

- Use reading aloud to reinforce good habits, but do this sensitively and in short chunks. Reading aloud helps embed sound-spelling links and aids vocabulary retention.

- Model correct stress and intonation, explaining how it works in the TL and draw slanting lines above written sentences to illustrate it.

- When using slides or other written words to illustrate sound-spelling links, highlight key sounds in a different colour.

- Talk about different accents in English, and contrast native language and TL sounds.

Some teachers like to do discrete phonics lessons, but my preference is to embed phonics within other communicative tasks, pausing now and again to focus on specific words and sounds. However you approach it, skilled teachers don't neglect pronunciation.

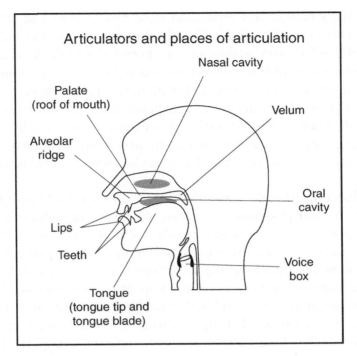

Figure 5.1 The vocal tract

Teaching listening

What does it mean to "teach listening"? I need to go into the theory just a little at this point. To listen effectively students use both **top-down** and **bottom-up** **processing**. What do these mean? Compare these scenarios:

Over dinner, a friend tells you a story about a recent holiday which went badly wrong. You listen with interest and make comments at appropriate moments, maybe to express surprise or sympathy.

The next day, a partner calls to ask you to buy some items at the supermarket for a meal. You listen carefully and make notes on a piece of paper.

How do you listen in each case? With the holiday, your main concern was probably understanding the general idea and knowing when a certain type of response was expected. In contrast, when listening to the shopping list, understanding the exact words was more important.

The way you listened to the holiday anecdote could be described as **top-down listening**. This refers to the use of background knowledge in understanding the meaning of the message and knowing how to react. Background knowledge involves context, i.e. the situation and topic, and what came before and after. Even the context of chatting casually to a friend limits the range of possible topics. Once the topic of a holiday has been established, our knowledge of the kind of things that can happen comes into play and helps us to match the incoming sounds against our expectations of what we might hear and to fill out specific details.

In contrast, when listening to the shopping list, comprehension is largely achieved by dividing and decoding the sound signal bit by bit. This is **bottom-up listening**. The ability to separate the stream of speech into separate words becomes more important if we're to recognise, for example, a brand of ketchup or a quantity of tomatoes.

To teach listening, therefore, we need to focus on both of these elements, but in particular, for our purposes as language teachers, on bottom-up processing. How do we help students recognise words and pick them out in the stream of sound? It's a really difficult thing to do without masses of practice, so the first thing to say about teaching listening is that you have to do lots of it! Secondly, if you want the main focus to be on bottom-up processing you need to do tasks which lay the emphasis on sound and vocabulary recognition and picking out words in the sound stream. Thirdly, it's usually better to work intensively on shorter aural texts than longer ones – you want to give students a sense of mastery. With that in mind, below are some activities that will aid the process.

- It sounds obvious, but make sure you teach vocabulary, words both in isolation and in context. Use the spoken word to do this, not just the written.

- Do transcription tasks, e.g. dictation of words, phrases and longer chunks, filling in letter gaps in words, completing notes on a grid while listening to instructions.

- Read aloud to students as they follow the written transcript.

- Recycle previously learned words and chunks as much as possible.

- Work intensively on short audio and video listening texts (see the next section, where a range of task types you can use are included).

- Listen to short statements and translate them into English.

- When doing question-answer work and other types of interaction, include the opportunity for students to write down answers to oral questions.

- Exploit the concept of "narrow listening", whereby the students are exposed, through different activities, to four or five short texts on the same topic and containing very similar vocabulary.

Really effective teachers recognise these issues and avoid seeing listening as a series of tests tacked on to a lesson, done "cold" without the preparation and practice needed to make them enjoyable and useful.

Using video listening

In real life we usually see the person we're listening too, so it's easier for students to listen if we create the same conditions. From the earliest stages of learning, the best source of listening is you the teacher, assuming that your skills are good (let's not forget that this is an important part of being an outstanding practitioner). When you're speaking you can tailor the level and speed of the TL to the class. You're the one best placed to know what students will understand. (This is why visiting speakers are often hard for students to understand since they don't have that detailed knowledge of your class's abilities.) **Most of the listening students do takes place when you are talking or interacting with them.** If your lessons are sequenced well, moving from easy to complex, scaffolding activities where necessary, your students will inevitably become better listeners.

When you need to use recorded material, video is therefore preferable to audio. An extra level of interest is created, with visual clues helping with meaning. In practice, many teachers, especially with beginners and intermediates, have to use audio alone since it's harder to source video at the right level, and professionally recorded video is expensive. With more advanced students, sources of video listening are abundant.

To exploit video bear in mind the following factors.

- Try not to go beyond three minutes in length (a bit more for advanced students) for intensive work.

- Choose clips based on clarity, interest and speed.

- In general avoid strong, non-standard accents.

The teaching sequence below is effective when using a video clip.

1) Do a pre-listening task, preparing students for the content they're going to hear. You could make sure you include some of the key vocabulary. This will arouse their interest, take advantage of their top-down skills, and get their minds on the task to come.

2) Tell students exactly what they'll have to do so that they know the purpose of the task.

3) Give them their worksheet task at the start, letting them see it while they're watching. This will improve the class's focus and support their listening.

4) Play the whole clip once without stopping. When you do this, remind them that listening places a huge load on their working memory, their "processing power", but not to worry, it will seem much easier by the end of the task.

5) Depending on the task, play the clip in short sections, repeatedly, or give them the means to do so if they're working independently. Observe the group carefully to adjust the number of times you need to repeat a section. Give your own verbal hints for more difficult sections or even say whole sections aloud if they're particularly hard.

6) Occasionally ask if they want to hear the section again.

7) Play the whole clip through at the end to enable students to check what they've written.

8) Get students to feed back their responses.

9) Where possible, provide a transcript at some point so they can see the text written down.

10) Do any appropriate follow-up work, e.g. oral discussion or general summary.

The above sequence works for audio too, of course. The point I'd make here is that a listening text (either video or audio) is often best exploited in some detail, in a very thorough manner since, as I've mentioned before, a listening text is both an excellent source of meaningful input, but also the basis for intensive input-output work.

Useful task types for audio and video listening include:

- true/false/not mentioned (including "not mentioned" is not only useful for assessment purposes – three responses are more reliable than just two – but it also gets students to listen even more carefully);

- ticking correct statements in TL or English (TL is better since it is a multi-skill task involving reading);

- correcting a faulty transcript (less demanding on comprehension since students have access to the written word, but good for listening to fine detail);

- gap-filling TL sentences (again, a multi-skill task like this is better for detail than a general comprehension task);

- gap-filling English statements (suitable for lower-attaining students);

- finding the French/German/Spanish for...;

- asking questions in TL (best for multi-skill practice);

- asking questions in English (easier, with a pure focus on comprehension);

- supplying a list of words for students to tick off when they hear them (useful, but may distract the students from general comprehension).

In addition it's worth noting that you need to make sure your students are prepared for the question types they'll encounter in exams. Research and experience show that familiarity with test type is a significant factor in achievement.

Teacher talk

In recent years teacher talk has become unfashionable in some quarters. It's certainly true that too much talk and too little student activity is undesirable, but in language teaching we've already shown how valuable teacher talk can be in providing TL input. Talking at length has its value too. In Box 5.1 are two simple, low-preparation, high-impact examples to demonstrate the point.

Box 5.1: "Detect my lies"

Give a simple account about yourself or, for example, what you did during the last weekend or a recent holiday. You can choose your topic depending on what theme, grammar or vocabulary you've recently covered. Simply talk for about two minutes and ask the class to detect five lies within your account. You could make these quite subtle inaccuracies or blindingly obvious inventions, depending on your class. Use as many verbal cues as possible to help students understand, e.g. repetition, rewording and hesitation.

Interview with a visitor

Your visitor might be a foreign language assistant, a native speaker visitor or even a colleague of yours. You interview the person for about 5–10 minutes, while the students either take notes or complete an information grid, including personal

---

details such as name, age, family, hobbies, films recently watched, favourite music, travel experiences, and so on. For this activity to be successful it's important that the visitor be primed in terms of how much language your class knows. If you show the person the information grid beforehand this helps greatly. The students report their answers to you or a partner.

Transcribing

Many effective teachers use transcribing and formal dictation to develop listening skills, grammatical competence and spelling. Dictation is very effective when you want your class to be particularly calm and focused, but you have to pitch it at the right level. It's very easy to make dictation too difficult, in which case it becomes dispiriting and counter-productive for all concerned. It's an excellent task for revision purposes, but only once structures and vocabulary have been taught and practised. As an exercise in pedagogical analysis consider the following, with regard to dictation.

Dictation or "running dictation"?

Running dictation, when you get students to work in pairs, with one partner fetching the text pinned up somewhere in the room and "delivering" to their partner, the scribe, is a popular task since students enjoy it and it keeps them physically active. But is it better than traditional teacher-led dictation?

In either form, dictation can be tailored very precisely to the class, as can the speed of delivery when you do it in the traditional way. It's particularly useful in French where the sound-spelling correspondences are more difficult than with, say, German or Spanish.

In favour of traditional dictation

- Students get to hear a better TL model. This means that students develop a better notion of the relationship between sounds, spellings, morphology and syntax.

- Student concentration may be good for long periods. It is usually useful for maintaining good behaviour.

- Students often say they enjoy it.

Against traditional dictation

● It may seem very passive. Some students find it so hard that they dislike doing it. Some teachers find it dull to administer.

● Although it involves listening and thinking, there's no speaking on the part of the students.

In favour of running dictation

● The students are speaking as well as listening.

● They get quite excited and competitive; it's fun for them.

● Because it's physically active it may suit restless students.

● The students collaborate, e.g. they spell out words to each other.

Against running dictation

● The students may hear poor models of pronunciation so develop a weak sense of sound/grammar/spelling relationships.

You may draw your own conclusions, but I'd consider using both approaches depending on whether you wish to emphasise the fun side or the "hard work" aspect. If I wanted to calm a class, I'd use formal dictation; if I wanted to excite the class, I'd do running dictation.

Of course, there are other ways of doing dictation, including simple paired dictation at the desk (which could be in the form of taking a phone message with students sitting back to back, to make it a little more fun). An idea to make dictation more accessible is to give students a sheet marked rather like this:

This gives them more clues to spelling when doing the task because the number of letters per word is indicated.

Teaching grammar through listening

One way to integrate listening within the teaching of other skills is to teach grammar through listening tasks. Here are three examples involving listening to bite-size chunks of language (with acknowledgement to Gianfranco Conti).

Sentence puzzles

Sentence puzzles are an effective way to teach grammar and syntax through listening. Provide students with a set of jumbled-up sentences to unscramble while you say them in the correct order. The task is to re-write them correctly in the table/grid provided, placing each element of the sentence under the right heading. After completing the transcribing task, ask students to work out the rule. In Table 5.1 are some sentence puzzles in French, followed by the grid.

Table 5.1 Sentence puzzles for teaching grammar through listening

| 1. suis allé stade je au ne jamais |
| 2. rien n' vu elle café au a |
| 3. sommes ne en nous pas taxi rentrés |
| 4. est restaurant on sorti au n' pas |
| 5. n' tu fait rien as ville en |

Personal pronoun	Negative	Auxiliary	Negative	Past participle	Preposition	Noun/ Pronoun
Je	ne	suis	jamais	allé	au	stade

Sorting tasks

Read aloud a number of sentences each containing a specific structure that you want students to notice. As they listen, students have to categorise the structure.

For example, you could work on tenses with intermediate or advanced classes by reading a series of sentences, each one featuring a different tense. Students simply tick off the tense they hear in each case from a list. A second example could focus on adjective endings in French. You read a series of statements, each one featuring the use of an adjective in its feminine form. Students note down whether the adjective is regular or irregular. Sorting tasks are easy to improvise and use as starters, fillers or plenaries.

"Find someone who"

Each student is given a card with fictitious details and a grid showing the details to look for. The task is to find people with those details on their cards by asking questions in the TL. Although it may appear to be a speaking task, this activity is mainly a listening one as students read out details in response to questions. Table 5.2 shows an example grid.

Table 5.2 "Find someone who" grid

Find someone who...	Name on card	Possible questions
never reads		What sports do you do? Do you read much?
goes out every evening		How often do you play computer games? Do you go out with your parents?
goes out with parents a lot		What do you do at the weekend?
never does sport		Do you watch much TV? How often do you go out?
no longer goes out		
does sport four times week		
reads every day		
plays computer games every day		
rarely watches TV		

What if my classes seem to be struggling with listening tests?

A common concern expressed by teachers is that their classes struggle with listening tests. This perception is partly due to the fact that, as we've seen, listening is a fleeting task, where students usually only get two chances to decode a lot of information. Panic can set in, minds go blank. Here are ten deliberately challenging questions which may suggest how to improve your students' listening performance.

1. Do you devote enough lesson time to some form of listening practice (including oral interaction tasks with you or a partner student)?

2. Are listening skills a main concern in your planning, both short and longer term? Do you put most of your effort into teaching vocabulary and grammar at the expense of building a bank of resources and a repertoire of strategies for listening?

3. Do your students perceive listening as crucial to their learning? Do you encourage them to practise listening independently?

4. Are you aware enough of the cognitive challenges your students face while listening, or learning to listen? When your students perform really poorly at a listening task, do you ask them what was hard?

5. Do you just stick to the textbook, pick tasks and press the play button following the teacher's book recommendations? Or do you adapt text book tasks to make them better learning opportunities? Do you plan for any pre- and post-listening tasks?

6. Do the texts you use contain comprehensible input, i.e. where the students already understand the large majority of the vocabulary and where the grammar doesn't pose major challenges?

7. Do the large majority of your listening activities consist of comprehension tasks? How often do you use listening activities to model new language in context, sentence construction and correct use of grammar and pronunciation?

8. How much do you focus in your lessons on training the students in bottom-up processing skills, especially decoding skills (how to turn a combination of letters into sounds) and any other skills which help students interpret the sound stream?

9. Do your students enjoy listening? Do you think of ways of making it more enjoyable, e.g. by video listening or including purposeful activities such as trying to spot mistakes or untruths in a message?

10. Do your students feel confident that they'll succeed? Do they say "Miss, I'm not good at listening"? If you've previously raised their own self-belief in this area they're more likely to be motivated to do the task.

Box 5.2: Tech tips

Try the **interactive video quizzes** provided by Ashcombe School, England (available at the time of writing). These are a series of simple interviews with native speakers, pitched at low-intermediate to intermediate level, along with associated gap-filling activities, which can be done online. Languages covered are French, German and Spanish.

Audio Lingua (audio-lingua.eu) has a large bank of audio clips spoken by native speakers. Languages covered include French, German, Spanish, Italian, Russian and Portuguese. You can listen online or download the files.

A **smartphone** is now a good source of audio material. At a simple level students can converse with their digital assistant, e.g. **Siri** (iPhone and iPad) or **Google Assistant** (Android/Google). **Amazon** devices and their assistant **Alexa** perform the same function. You can set students a series of TL questions to ask their phone or tablet the answers, which they can transcribe. In addition, advanced-level students can download the app **TuneIn Radio**, or similar, which will let them listen to TL speech radio. You need to make sure, however, that students are aware that radio broadcasts will seem very fast so they'll have to persevere. The **News in Slow French** site offers reports at a slower pace together with transcriptions, and there are equivalents for other languages.

The brilliant **Lyrics Training** site links to pop videos in various languages. You listen to the song and complete a gap-fill task at the bottom of the page. As you write the most recent line of the song repeats itself to give you time to check before you move on. I'd recommend this strongly for advanced-level classes who wish to do enjoyable independent work.

Text-to-speech apps allow students to copy and paste or type in texts which can then be listened to. They are useful when students have to prepare presentations or memorised answers to questions. **Voki** is a well-known app of this type.

> **Set a listening task** from the internet, preferably with a specific worksheet. You choose the source based on interest and language level. You can check the task is done by issuing a paper or electronic worksheet.

Concluding remarks

It's worth noting that the very best way to see a quantum leap in your students' listening performance is if they have the opportunity for an immersion experience, preferably in the TL country. The best teachers try to make this possible whenever circumstances allow. You nearly always see significantly improved listening test scores from students who have recently spent time on a family exchange.

Let's be clear: listening skills can't be quickly fixed; you can't teach them like a point of grammar or a list of vocabulary. They take years to develop through masses of exposure, carefully graded input, practice at strategies and interaction. If you focus on them from the start it's more likely your classes will perform well in the future.

Chapter 6

Purposeful games

Introduction

Games are a staple of language lessons, allowing teachers to use the TL in a uniquely enjoyable way. I'll offer a rationale for effective games followed by a description of a number of games which maximise both learning and enjoyment. Effective teachers use games selectively and only when there's a clear pedagogical benefit, allowing for stimulating recycling of language. They're aware of what's known in economics as "opportunity cost", i.e. the loss of other alternatives when one alternative is chosen. So if you play a game, what else might you have done instead which may have been more educationally valuable? In other words, what's the return on investment?

Bear in mind that games or game-like activities are just another example of language tasks with a purpose, so there's no need to belittle their value. The unique element they offer, however, is a degree of amusement or competition which adds an edge, an extra source of motivation. After learning and practising new vocabulary or structures, students have the opportunity to use the TL in a non-stressful, purposeful way. While playing games, the students' attention is on the message, less on the form of the language. Let's look at how to exploit a few well-known games.

Battleships with a twist

This familiar paired game is useful for **near-beginner** and **low-intermediate** students, is familiar to most language teachers and is commonly used to practise and embed knowledge of verb conjugations. Each pair has a rectangular grid, typically with about eight cells across and six down. Table 6.1 shows an example for practising regular present tense –*er* verbs in French:

Table 6.1 Battleships grid

	jouer	regarder	dessiner	parler	chanter	écouter	travailler
Je		▨					
Tu		▨		▨	▨		
Il/Elle							
On							
Nous			▨				
Vous	▨					▨	▨
Ils/Elles	▨						

Students are paired up and instructed to shade in, say, five ships, each consisting of two horizontal or vertical cells (as in Table 6.1). It's best to do this in English to avoid any confusion and to get the task going quickly. Needless to say, each student must not show their grid to their partner. Then tell students they should take it in turns to guess where their partner's ships are. To do so they must give a correctly conjugated form of the verb, e.g. *nous écoutons*. The partner replies by saying in TL *hit* or *miss*. The winner is the first to discover all their partner's ships. It's a good idea to advise students how to keep a record of their hits and misses, stressing that this is a game of skill, not just pot luck.

It's wise to use this game later in a teaching sequence about present tense *–er* verbs and, of course, the game has its limitations since it focuses on grammatical form and has little, if any, real communicative value. However, most teachers would argue that the repeated use of each verb form (just think how many times students utter and hear the verbs) will help students use them automatically in the future.

If you want to add a greater communicative value to the task, suppose you are working on the past (preterite) tense with a grid made up of pronouns down the left and infinitives along the top. Normally you would get students to just give the pronoun and verb, e.g. in German *du hast getanzt* (you danced). Instead, you can require them to add an extra element to the verb, so a student might say *du hast mit deinem Freund getanzt*. At some point during the game you can then ask students to make up sentences with a verb + two extra elements, e.g. *du hast gestern mit deinem Freund getanzt*. In this case an important aspect of German word order (time/manner/place of adverbs) is practised. Some time later you can get them to add another element to their sentences, e.g. make the sentences negative. The challenge of adding extra elements provides a natural progression to the lesson and some enjoyment for students as their creativity is challenged.

Incidentally, Battleships can also work well with vocabulary. For example, near-beginner students could use their grid to design a simple town with, say, one square for a shop, two for a railway station, two for a swimming pool, three for a shopping centre, etc. To make this game more challenging you could require them to add a verb to the place, thus practising, in French, *aller* with *au/à la/aux*, e.g. *je vais à la gare*. In pairs it would work like this: *Tu vas à la piscine? Non, je ne vais pas à la piscine. Tu vas au stade? Oui, je vais au stade.* Intermediate students could use their grid to design a campsite in order to practise terms such as *pitch, games area, restaurant, reception, toilets*, etc.

Simon Says

This is a quintessentially successful game format for **near-beginner** and **intermediate** levels. Just in case you're unfamiliar with it, the class stands up, you instruct the students to touch parts of their body, usually preceding the instruction with the words *Simon says* (TL equivalent). If you don't say *Simon says* they mustn't touch that part of their body. When a student makes a mistake they sit down.

To run the game successfully you normally play it sometime after you've taught parts of the body, but it can be used to teach body parts for the first time. Before the game proper begins you should have the students stand and follow your instructions to touch parts of their bodies. Once the game starts you'd be wise to let a few students make mistakes before they're penalised. Make sure you maintain eye contact and scan the class front to back, side to side.

The speed at which you go depends on the class, but if you've played the game yourself you'll know how much concentration it requires! The number of body parts you focus on depends on the class. The particular value of the game, which makes it a classic, is that students hear the words for *ears, eyes, head, hand*, etc, numerous times, helping to fix them in long-term memory. Lots of language is learned, there's a clear goal and plenty of enjoyment.

Cryptic vocabulary quiz

This reading game can be used at any level, but is maybe best at **near-beginner** or **low-intermediate** level. Choose a theme such as famous personalities, actors or even teachers' names. Then make up nonsense words or chunks which, when translated literally, tell you who the person is. For example, in French *M. Forgeron* would be Mr Smith or, more inventively, the pop band *Pièce de Froideur* or female singer *Dame Folle* could be used. (I'll let you work those out.) This game provides a good opportunity for practice at using the dictionary.

Bingo games

Here are some examples of useful, enjoyable games for **beginners** and **intermediate** level students which, by their great use of repetition, help fix TL numbers in students' minds. In passing, note that having students speak numbers in order (1–10) has limited value, since in nearly all communicative contexts numbers need to be uttered and recognised instantly and not in relation to their order, so any task which requires random recall or production of numbers is useful. It's helpful to have a stock of real bingo cards in your cupboard to add a touch of extra interest and authenticity. You could also invest in a bingo machine for the same reason.

Mental arithmetic bingo

Instead of reading out a number, give classes a simple mental arithmetic sum to solve which leads to a number that may be on their card. You'll need to teach them simple terms like *plus, minus, multiplied by* and *divided by*. The advantage of this variation is that it provides more mental challenge. The downside is that students don't make the immediate link between the numbers you read and the number on their card. You might also need quite a quick-thinking class to do it.

Reverse bingo

In this variation all the class stands up. Call out numbers and if one comes up which is on a student's card, they must sit down and they're out of the game. This variation goes by quite quickly and is a fun alternative, but the obvious downside is that once a student is out they have no more motivation to listen to the numbers. In this case, you can ask them to write down the numbers anyway. You could play reverse bingo after traditional bingo to provide a twist to the lesson.

Word bingo

Write up on the board about 15 to 20 words you wish to revise and ask students to select five of them. Then either read aloud the words or, for greater challenge, give definitions of each word. The first student to tick off their five words wins.

Number sequence bingo

Instead of just reading a number, read simple sequences of numbers and students have to work out what the next number would have been. You can make this as simple or as hard as you want, depending on the class. e.g. 1, 2, 3, 4 __. Or 64, 32, 16 __. You can cater for any number easily, e.g. 5, 4, 3, 2 __. I like this version because students get to hear a lot of numbers, so you're maximising the input. The minor downside is that, as in mental arithmetic bingo, students don't immediately match the number they hear and the one on their card.

Group bingo

Break the class into small groups and get one person to act as caller. This has the advantage of allowing some students to do the calling. The downside is that students may hear poorer models of pronunciation and there's the danger of an over-noisy classroom.

Number in a sentence bingo

In this variation, instead of reading out a number, you read a sentence containing the number, e.g. in Spanish *Hay treinta alumnos en la clase* (There are thirty students in the class). This offers a greater level of challenge and is an opportunity to provide input at sentence level, allowing students to hear the numbers in context. Some classes may find it too hard and you may need to do a bit of thinking beforehand about the nature of the sentences which are feasible.

TL quiz games

One of my favourite "go-to" end of term games for **advanced** level students is a version of the British TV quiz game for students, University Challenge. The class is divided into two or more groups of about four students. You need to prepare at least a hundred general knowledge questions grouped by theme, all relating to the TL culture, e.g. food, history, art, cultural icons, geography, music and language. Ask a starter question for ten points, and the first team to answer correctly on the buzzer gets the right to answer three more follow-up questions on the same topic. If a student incorrectly answers before the question is finished they lose five points and the question passes over to a member of the opposing team. Conferring is allowed between team members for the follow-up questions.

Purposeful games

This game works on more than one level. The students have to listen hard to large amounts of TL input in order to understand the questions while learning lots of information about the TL country. You get to control the pace of the language and the difficulty level of questions. You can use multiple-choice questions to make answers more accessible and provide even more input.

A second quiz game which works well for **intermediate** level is The Price is Right. If you aren't familiar with it, contestants have to guess the price of items they're presented with. This is easy to run with a class. Prepare by making a PowerPoint presentation with about 20 different items you've found in online stores. Keep a list of the prices. The more interesting you can make the items from a cultural standpoint, the better. You could, of course, choose items related to a recent topic you've been working on.

Invite four students up to the board at a time, describe the item they can see displayed, tailoring your language to the needs of the class, then ask each contestant to name a price in euro. The student closest to the actual price gets to stay up for the next round. You can see that the main value of this game is really listening; no bad thing. An alternative twist would be to display three items at once, describe them, then give a price for one of the three. The contestants have to identify the correct item. To make sure all the class is involved you can get them to write down their own guesses on a mini-whiteboard.

Categories

This vocabulary building game goes by various names and can be used with **near-beginners** and **intermediate** students. It's the one where you give students a grid such as Table 6.2 with categories across the top and letters down the left-hand side.

Table 6.2 Categories

	School	Animals	Food	Countries	Home	Sports	Clothes
M							
P							
T							
A							
B							

You can play this in a number of ways.

- Give the students the whole grid and within a time limit, either individually or in pairs, they have to find a word in each category beginning with the letter shown. They may or may not use dictionaries. The former tests memory, the latter improves dictionary use skills and teaches new language.

- Give the students just one letter at a time and a strict time limit, say two minutes. The individual or pair gets two points for a word no-one else gets, or one point for a word which others have also found.

- As above, but allow students to include as many words as they can find for each letter. They may well need a dictionary for this.

Bear in mind that the biggest challenge of this game is correcting the answers as this can become too noisy if not tightly controlled.

Alibi

This is a winner for **intermediate** and **advanced** groups. Tell the class that a crime was committed in the town last night at 8.00. (Make it plausible, e.g. a mugging or a burglary.) Explain in dead-pan fashion that there are two suspects. Then say that the suspects are thought to come from this school and it's even thought they come from this classroom. At this point a few students will see that you're joking (many will not, however!).

Then explain that you're going to ask for two volunteers who'll leave the room for five minutes to make up an alibi. Stress that they must prepare in great detail in order to explain what they were doing together the previous night. They should have a common story, e.g. cinema visit, meal or night at a friend's house.

While the two volunteers are out of the room, prepare TL questions with the rest of the group. You can put these on the board so students can read from them later, if necessary. Questions will include: *What were you doing last night at 8.00? What were you wearing? What was the weather like? How did you get to the cinema?* etc. You need to stress that the class must look for details.

After five minutes the first volunteer returns to the room to be questioned in mock courtroom style, e.g. get the student to swear an oath on the dictionary or textbook. (The second student has to wait patiently outside for about ten minutes.) After questioning the first suspect, get the second one to come in for their interrogation. This is when the fun starts as the class discovers if the two stories tally.

At the end of the second interrogation ask students to sum up any discrepancies and to vote on whether the couple are guilty or innocent. The whole activity takes about 30 minutes or so and involves practice of past tenses. You can decide if you wish to place much emphasis on grammatical accuracy. In any case, as you contribute to the questioning and pass comment, students will receive plenty of high quality, graded listening input as well as an opportunity to practise question forms.

What can I take on holiday?

This is based on a parlour game you might have come across at parties and would work with **intermediate** to **advanced** level. (It could be adapted for **near-beginners** if you list lots of vocabulary on the board.) I'm grateful to Martina Bex (see Bibliography) for reminding me of this game. I've adapted her description.

Tell students that they're going on a holiday and have to work out what they can or can't take with them. Only you know the criterion that an object must meet for the student to be able to take it. The students must work out the criterion (see possible criteria below).

Give students one example of an object which can be taken, enclosed in a model TL statement, e.g. *I'm going to Barcelona, and I'm going to bring [a swimsuit]*. Write the model statement on the board, then turn it into a question and reflect it back to the class: *What are you going to bring to Barcelona?*

After each suggestion from the students, you say *Yes, you can* or *No, you can't*. Gradually students will work out the trick but, if they don't, you can give hints or more models of right and wrong answers to make it more obvious. Providing absurd examples makes the game more engaging still.

Here are three possible criteria you can use to play the game:

- The first is the hardest and most fun. You must say *Um* or *Uh* before you make the statement, e.g. *Um ... I'm going to Barcelona and I'm going to bring a castle*. In order for this to work well it's best if you use no hands up as opposed to having students raise their hands. If the students have planned out what they're going to say, they won't often say *Um*. Your students who are excellent at public speaking may get frustrated because they don't use fillers, so they won't ever be allowed to bring the items they suggest.

- The items must go in alphabetical order, e.g. *I'm going to Barcelona, and I'm going to bring an apple; I'm going to Barcelona, and I'm going to bring a boat; I'm going to Hawaii, and I'm going to bring some cheese.* You can make it less obvious by not starting with the letter "a" or by using words the initial letters of which are disguised in sound, like (in English) "xylophone" or "photos".

- The items must all consist of the same number of letters: food, door, cars, hand, etc. You would need to plan a list of these ahead of time for you to use as examples, because it isn't easy to think of them on the spot.

Below are some possible patterns you could use if you want to use the game to rehearse grammatical structures.

- *I go to __ and I bring __.*

- *I'm going to go to __ and I'm going to bring __.*

- *I want to go to __ and I want to bring __.*

- *I'm thinking about going to __ and I'm thinking about bringing __.*

- *I went to __ and I brought __.*

- *If I were to go to __, I would bring __.*

- *When I used to go to __, I used to bring __.*

- *When you go to __, I recommend that you bring __.*

Another scenario you could employ for this game is travel destinations to practise prepositions – *I'm taking the plane to … um … Paris, but I'm not taking the plane to London.*

Silly story writing

This is for **intermediate** to **advanced** level. You pair up students and give them a sheet of A3 paper each. Begin by calling out a category (e.g. the name of a town in the TL country) and giving the students a minute to write down as many words as they can from that category. Do another four categories, e.g. animals, means of transport, furniture and famous people from the history of the country. Don't tell the students what will follow; leave them wondering what's going on. You can then elicit some brief feedback from pairs. *What words did you find?*

Next, tell them that they have 15 minutes to write a brief story which incorporates all the words they wrote down. Tell them the story can be as weird as they like, but they should try to be as grammatically accurate as possible. Explain that when the 15 minutes is up, you'll ask pairs at random to read their story aloud (this should add some urgency to the task). When the 15 minutes have elapsed invite a selection of pairs to read their story aloud.

A variation on this game is to get students to choose just one word from each category and write a five sentence mini-story where each sentence contains one word from their list. This can even be done as a whole-class task, but in this format a smaller group would make more sense.

Answers on the board

This is for **intermediate** to **advanced** level. Write five to ten pieces of information about yourself on the board as very short answers to personal questions, e.g. *Three* (for *How many sisters do you have?* or any other question to which *three* is the true answer) and *London* (for *Where were you born?* or any other suitable question such as *What was the last city you visited?*). Students score one point for each question they ask that gets an answer which is written on the board, until all the answers have been ticked off. If they ask a question which has a different answer from the one on the board, you just answer the question, e.g. *None* for *How many brothers do you have?* or *Manchester* for *Where do your parents live?* Students can continue the game in groups, preparing their answers on blank paper before they start asking questions orally one at a time as they think of them.

This game would fit very well towards the end of a sequence of work about question formation. A student could easily take over your role from the front of the class, or, once the game has been played as a whole class, groups of students could then play on their own.

Me too!

For **intermediate** to **advanced** level. In pairs, students try to find things they have in common with each other by asking questions they think their partner will answer with something that is true for both of them. If they have the same opinion, they can react with *Me too!* or *Me neither!* and score one point. For example, if they ask *What's your favourite subject?* and their partner answers with the same favourite subject, they can say *Me too!* and score one point. This can be good practice of language such as *can* or *have you ever*, and is an effective ice-breaker or a great way of improving classroom dynamics by emphasising what students have in common. Before or during the game, you might want to teach suitable language for reacting when the answer is something that's not true for the person asking the question (and therefore doesn't score a point), e.g. *Really? I don't* and *Really? My favourite…*

Mr and Mrs

For **intermediate** to **advanced** level. This is similar in principle to the Alibi game described above and based on a familiar TV format. Once again it's a good way of practising question forms. Get two students to volunteer to be the couple and send them out of the room for five to ten minutes to find out as much as possible about each other. It helps if the pair are already friends. While they are outside preparing, you revise question forms with the rest of the class and write up some model questions on the board to which the class can refer. Questions will be in the third person, e.g. *What is her favourite colour? Where did she go on holiday last summer? What's her favourite sport? Who is her favourite movie actor?*

The "married couple" come in one by one to be interrogated by the class. The winner is the one who gets the most correct answers. Note that, as with Alibi, although at any one moment only one student will be speaking, the whole class will be listening to what you and the other class members say. This is, therefore, an excellent listening activity above all.

Grammar auction

This is a popular and useful error correction game which can be used with **all levels**. Students bid for the right to say whether a sentence is right or wrong and/ or correct it, doubling the money they bid if they're right and losing that money if they're wrong. There are variations of this game, but one approach is to split the class into two teams and give each team a sum of money, say 1 million euro.

You then display a sentence which is either correct or contains one or more errors. You could even make them up as you go along if you think the teams are winning or losing too much money and depending on your class's ability to spot errors. One member of each team volunteers to place their bet while someone keeps a tally of the gains and losses.

One way of making sure one team doesn't dominate or get left out is to stop the game after a certain number of questions, "save" the money they have at that point, and then give each team an equal amount of money to bid with from then on. This can be repeated three or four times, and then all the saved amounts added together for their final score.

A limitation of this activity is that relatively little TL is being used and there is little or no TL communication (although teams might discuss in English), but if the sentences are well designed by the teacher, they're a good basis for general discussion of grammar points.

Would I lie?

For intermediate to **advanced** levels. Students try to work out which three of six statements are not true by asking you questions. Prepare six statements about yourself, three true and three false, and write them on the board. For example:

- *My brother has twin sons.*

- *I have three cats.*

- *If I'd been a boy, I would've been called George.*

- *My family was brought up in Spain.*

- *My favourite movie is The Sound of Music.*

- *My father was an extra in Star Wars.*

You ask the class how many of the statements they think are false. Then tell them there are three and they have to work out which are false by asking you questions, listening to your answers and watching your reaction. You can embroider your answers as much as possible, giving the right number of hints depending on how fast you think your class is.

Let the students ask questions until they've decided which ones they believe (by a show of hands). Give them the real answer. You could add an element of competition by putting the class into pairs or small groups, with each grouping coming up with their chosen three false statements. An extension to this task is to ask students to write down similar statements for themselves – three true and three false. Divide them into groups and repeat as above with one person from the group being questioned by the others.

One lie

While on the theme of being economical with the truth, here's another game for **intermediate** level students that can be played in pairs. Give students about five minutes to write down a set of statements about themselves, all of which are true except one. In turn, each student reads their sentences and their partner has to identify the false statement. You can make this fit a particular grammar point you've been working on, e.g. to practise the past (preterite) tense you could set the them *What I did last summer?* Or, to practise the future tense *My plans for the future*. A simple variation would be for each student to discover how many lies their partner told, rather than just find one.

Miming games

These can work at **all levels**, depending on the variation.

1. Vocabulary mimes

Students mime a word they choose or are given, without speaking or using sound effects, until their partners say exactly that word. This works particularly well for adjectives, adverbs, action verbs and idiomatic phrases such as body part idioms: *My head aches*, etc.

2. Sentence mimes

This is similar to vocabulary mimes, but students have to mime and guess whole sentences, e.g. *The lion jumped over the chair*. These sentences can be given by you, taken from a textbook exercise or text, written by the person or group that is going to mime, or written by another group as a challenge.

3. Imperfect tense mimes

Students mime actions to each other in pairs. While one partner is miming their partner says *Stop!* and then explains to them what they were in the process of doing. The imperfect tense is required to give the explanation, e.g. *you were making a cup of tea*, *you were watching a scary movie* or *you were brushing your teeth*.

Snakes and ladders

This simple board game generates lots of conversational TL at **all levels**. Design a board and on every two or three spaces write a TL question, either based on your current topic or for general review or preparation for an assessment. Students work in pairs and engage in conversations by asking and answering questions when they land on question spaces. This is an example of how a simple twist to a basic activity (asking general questions) makes it more enjoyable. Another good example of this is the widely used task speed dating where students ask each other questions in pairs, changing partners every three minutes.

Call my bluff

An **advanced** level game played with a panel of three versus the rest of the class. For each round the panel in turn reads a different definition of an unusual word selected by the teacher. Only one definition is correct, the other two are bluffs. After each panellist has read out their definition students choose what they believe to be the correct definition. The class may ask questions to each panellist to see how well they can improvise around their definition. Do they sound convincing or not? Brief the panellists in advance to be inventive. You need this activity to be more than just reading aloud and listening.

Provide each panellist with a card showing the words TRUE and FALSE in TL to hold up when the class has finally voted for the correct answer. The class collects points for correct guesses. The panel can remain the same for each round or be rotated.

Box 6.1: Tech tips

There are plenty of online language games, but be very selective when it comes to classroom use. Below are three I can recommend.

- **The Language Gym** (language-gym.com) has free verb conjugation and vocabulary games. These can make useful starters or be used for review of previously learned language.

- **Languages Online** (languagesonline.org.uk) has free Spellmaster and Quizlet vocabulary games which will reinforce previous learning.

- **Taskmagic** (mdlsoft.co.uk) is a commercial site with a range of attractive games which allow you to input your own language, tailored to your classes.

Print-Bingo.com and **Bingobaker.com** are free bingo card generators.

This site from **SUNY Cortland** has an enormous archive of games and game-like activities: http://web.cortland.edu/flteach/FAQ/FAQ-Activities.html

---

Concluding remarks

Great language teachers don't have to play games, but most do. If your class's behaviour is good, students use their time fruitfully and there's a clear learning aim, games can be a very useful tool in your kit. It's usually best to keep them simple so that not too much time is spent preparing materials or explaining complex rules that some students won't understand. If a game involves preparing cards, make sure you laminate them or at the very least keep them for future use. Games are also great to have available as activities to fall back on if something goes wrong with your planned lesson – the computer fails or the photocopier gets jammed.

There also needs to be an element of mental as well as linguistic challenge in any game you play. If a game goes well, quieter students may emerge from their shell and students leave your lesson thinking "that was fun" – probably a good thing. One last point: try to avoid having just one winner if you can, e.g. with bingo, continue calling after the first person has ticked off all their numbers or words. Younger students can be genuinely disappointed if they lose!

Chapter 7

Getting grammatical

Introduction

How much grammar should you teach? How should you do it best? This chapter considers what it means to "teach grammar". Effective teachers spend some time teaching rules, but make their clear priority the use of grammar, "knowing" the language, not just "knowing about" the language. There isn't much point in a student being able to describe a rule if they can't apply or comprehend it in real situations. I'll show that you can have the best of both worlds in the languages classroom: you can provide lots of meaningful input as well as doing controlled grammar practice. I'll give some examples of how best to use worksheets and create opportunities for structured practice of grammar, including through the use of digital technology. Finally, when some syllabuses place a larger emphasis on grammatical accuracy, what can outstanding teachers do to prepare their students for tasks such as translation?

To begin with, here's an example of one approach to teaching a verb tense, along with a detailed commentary.

Teaching the imperfect tense at low-intermediate level

Begin by telling students in English that today's class is really important because they're going to learn a new verb tense. Try to create a sense of occasion! Tell them to listen hard as you talk about pictures on the board (Figure 7.1). Ask them to try and notice something in the way you pronounce the words.

Then describe the pictures to the class in the TL. Make a point of clearly uttering the different verb forms.

In 1990 Johnny Incredible lived in a flat, he used to ride a bicycle to work, he used to drink beer and he used to eat fries. He used to wear jeans and a T-shirt. He was a taxi driver.

Figure 7.1 Imperfect and present tense pictures

Now, in 201... he lives in a mansion and he drives a Rolls Royce. He drinks champagne every day and eats steak and caviar. He often wears a tuxedo and he is a famous rock star.

Some smarter students will be noticing your verbs forms already, although many will be mainly focused on the meaning and pictures.

Next, run through the pictures again, this time immediately juxtaposing the past and the present.

In 1990 Johnny used to live in a flat, now he lives in a mansion, and so on.

At this point you could already ask in English what the students noticed about the verbs. Alternatively, you could save this and begin exploiting the pictures further as described in Table 7.1.

If you hadn't pointed out what was going on grammatically before, now would be a good time to do so. Try asking: "Does anyone think they know what we're doing here?" This would be my preference: to let students work things out for themselves through examples. (Actually, there's no clear research evidence that this is the best way, so if you prefer just to explain the rule first, then work through the oral practice, that's fine.)

In line with the recurring theme of this book, the above routine, lasting about 20 minutes, involves intensive recycling of the key language and doesn't confuse students by including irrelevant material. This is what I mean by "teaching grammar" – presenting and using a structure in a meaningful context. Explaining a rule alone with little or no practice is of little use. Allowing students to build up their automaticity through a structured routine such as the above, gives them a much greater chance of embedding their skill and knowledge. A classic challenge for creative teachers is to come up with ways to practise grammar which are both enjoyable and productive. Some students will accept almost any approach to learning and applying a new rule, but most need something extra to engage them.

All this is strongly rooted in the PPP (Presentation-Practice-Production) approach which is well-established in language teaching methodology. You show examples, get students to do controlled practice, then give them freedom to use the structure for themselves. Through this repetitive process you hope that students will gradually be able to use the structure for themselves in an unrehearsed situation.

I'd add one other point: for classroom routines such as those described above to be effective, students need to be in the habit of following them. This calls for a degree of consistency on your part. If students are used to your way of working they're much more likely to play the game, the rules of which they know. Be prepared at any stage to explain what you're doing and why. Ask them: "Why do you think I'm teaching you this tense in this way?"

Table 7.1 Imperfect tense teaching sequence

Teacher	Student(s)	Commentary
Hide the pictures depicting the past and ask: *Does Johnny live in a flat or a mansion? Where does he live? Does he drive a Mini? What type of car does he drive?* etc.	Hands up and occasional no hands up. *He lives in a mansion. He drives a Rolls Royce.*	Mix up your question types, using yes/no, either/or and open questions. Adjust this to the speed of your class and their usual expectation. Throw occasional questions at non-volunteers, get individuals to repeat correct responses.
Hide the present tense pictures and display the imperfect tense ones. Repeat the above routine.	As above.	As above. Be prepared to recast incorrect verb forms and any other errors.
Reveal the two columns of pictures together again. Mix up past and present questions.	As above. Use choral repetition when you think it will help "fix" the verb forms or endings.	Intermediate groups will do group repetition if they are trained into it. It keeps everyone on the ball and they can find it amusing at this level.
Now, leaving all the pictures displayed, tell the class you are not going to ask a question, just point at a picture. They will have to give a response.	Students give responses. Hands up.	This subtle change of activity changes the mood in the lesson and allows you to repeat the same work in a slightly different way. This is a key principle to remember; "same, but different".
Pair up students and ask each partner to describe the two columns of pictures to their partner. The partner may correct.	Students try to recreate your original commentary in pairs.	Another change of perspective to the lesson, building the level of challenge.
Ask an individual to summarise in full either one column or both.	Hands up.	Get two or three students to do the task. This allows you to let the best students stretch themselves. It's a minor example of effective "differentiation by task".
Reveal a written version of the commentary and read it aloud once more.	Students listen and read.	This allows students still in any doubt to see the different verb forms and spellings they may have been curious to see.

Making rules stick

If you want students to develop any independence and proficiency in speech and writing they have to acquire the basic patterns of grammar to some extent and not just be able to explain rules. This is a major challenge if you have only limited time with your classes. Even so, as we've seen, students will only pick up the rules and use them with some fluency if they've had the chance to see them in action and practise using them. Explanation takes the least time; it's hearing and reading many examples of grammar in use, then having a go at practising them that leads to results. If you don't provide these elements the grammar won't be picked up.

Below is a three-part template you might choose to follow and which provides a slightly different perspective, one rooted in skill-acquisition theory. (I'm grateful to Gianfranco Conti for many of the points here.)

1. Modelling and awareness-raising

In the first stage you model the TL structure and demonstrate the differences between English and second language usage. This is the equivalent of the Presentation phase in the PPP model.

You can lighten the cognitive load for students if necessary as follows.

- Use English to explain the rule, unless it's really simple.

- Produce examples containing language with which the students are very familiar, i.e. don't include new vocabulary.

- Avoid forcing students to practise orally unless they're particularly able.

- Provide translations of the examples for clarity and to help the students compare with English.

- Avoid exceptions to the rule you're presenting.

You may decide to use a **deductive** or an **inductive** approach. In the deductive approach, you explain the structure and give examples. In the inductive approach, on the other hand, you show the students examples of the structure in use and ask them to work out the rules by themselves. You can give hints along the way to help. Inductive teaching involves problem solving and greater cognitive investment in the process, which means it may lead to better retention. The deductive approach is quicker and better suits more complex structures.

2. Receptive processing

This may be neglected by some teachers, who move straight to spoken practice at this stage. This may work with the more able students, but others need to hear and read many more models before they have a chance to produce examples themselves. Why is this?

- Listening and reading are less demanding, especially when effective support or scaffolding is provided.

- If the texts you use contain language the students are familiar with, this provides old material onto which to hook the new items, and may make it easier for students to remember.

- Examples in context are more meaningful to students than random examples. These could relate to your current topic, your school, teachers or to individuals in the class.

- Reading allows more time for students to process the new information whereas production puts more cognitive and emotional pressure on them.

- Modelling through listening, with a transcript of the text, can be valuable in preventing many decoding and pronunciation errors that may impede learning. (See Chapter 5 for more on using listening to teach grammar.)

Reading tasks

These can include:

- **grammar judgement quizzes** such as **"right or wrong?"** – students are asked to decide, working alone or in groups, if a sentence is wrong or right and explain why;

- **"spot the correct one"** – two, three or four sentences are given which have the same intended meaning but only one is correct; students have to spot it and explain why it's correct;

- **gap-filling tasks with options**;

- **sentence reordering tasks** – the words in a sentence are randomly and incorrectly arranged and students have to place them in the right order;

- **text searches** – students find as many instances as possible of a certain structure in a series of short texts and translate the sentences that contain them either orally or in writing;

Getting grammatical

- **error identification and correction** – students are given a set of sentences, some of which are right and some of which contain one mistake involving the target structure; they must identify the mistakes, then explain and correct them;

- **short text translations** – can be done in a number of ways: (1) write a TL sentence on the whiteboard and students translate on mini-whiteboards to a time limit; (2) in groups students are given a set of sentences to translate; (3) read the sentence and students translate using mini-whiteboards or paper (note that mini-whiteboards allow you to see more clearly how students are doing);

- **"narrow reading" texts with comprehension tasks** – students are given a small number of short texts, each one featuring similar syntax, thus ensuring that they encounter the same language several times, helping it stick in their minds.

Listening tasks

These are important, as incorrect pronunciation of grammatical features can cause problems. For example, in French, the common mistake of voicing the silent "e" in the ending of the first person of the present tense (e.g. *je parle*) can sound like the first person of the imperfect (*je parlais*), etc.

- **Gapped dictations** are an effective way of checking if students have picked up sound decoding skills and to raise awareness of how the gapped elements fit in a sentence, e.g. the word order of adjectives in French, Spanish and Italian.

- **Paired reading aloud with translation and/or critical listening**, e.g. (1) Translation: students read short texts to each other and translate orally what they hear their partner say and (2) Critical listening: students listen to and correct the pronunciation of the key words involved in the grammar point being taught.

- **"Narrow listening" with comprehension tasks**. You read a few short paragraphs, each one featuring examples of the key grammar and similar vocabulary.

3. Structured production

When you think students are ready you could move on to spoken and written tasks. Note that you might be able to move to these more quickly with higher-achieving classes.

Oral tasks

- **Sentence builders.** Students, working in pairs, give each other sentences in English to translate into the TL using a "sentence builder", i.e. a frame featuring elements the students could use to build up sentences.

- **Cue cards.** Prepare a deck of cards with English sentences to translate and students take turns in picking a card and translating. Students could work in groups of three, taking turns to be the referee; the most accurate player wins.

- **Communicative drills**, e.g. give students prompts in the TL and they have to make a simple adjustment or transformation to your prompt:
  Teacher: *Last weekend I played football.*
  Student: *Last weekend I played tennis.*
  Drills like this are easy to make up on the spot and make great starters or plenaries.

- **"Find someone who..."**, using cards. Students are given a card with a fictitious name and details. The task is to find eight to ten friends with specific details on their cards. Students go around asking questions in order to find the information. The cards feature the grammar point you want students to practise. (See Chapter 5.)

- **Pictures or flashcards.** These can act as a prompt to produce speech featuring your target grammar, e.g. you show a sport and the students say *I played...* to practise the past tense.

Written tasks

- **Parallel texts with partial translation.** Give students parallel texts in English and the TL, where the TL version is gapped; the gaps are placed where the target structure is used in order to focus on its application in the text.

- **Gap-filling tasks,** e.g. provide incomplete sentences or passages with gaps to fill. These work well with verb forms and adjectives.

- **Translations** into the TL.

- **Sentence-combining tasks.** Two sentences are given and students have to blend them into one new sentence using the target structure. Example: *My mother is 42. She is a lawyer. She really enjoys her job.* If the target structure is relative pronouns the cue is: *who, whom, which* or *where.* The combined sentence could be: *My mother, who is 42, works as a lawyer and really enjoys her job.*

- **Picture tasks.** Students describe a picture making up sentences which include the target structure. You can provide some scaffolding to help. A complex scene could be used to practise prepositions, for example.

- **Short essays with prompts**. Get students to write a short essay with bulleted prompts that closely guide them on what to write, inviting use of the TL structure(s).

Lesson planning tips

- Narrow down the focus of your grammar lesson as much as possible; avoid sources of confusion.

- Consider interference from English and the mistakes commonly made by the average student you teach. How can you avoid them happening? Ask the question: "Is it better to highlight the contrast between the two languages, or will this cause greater confusion?" I would lean towards highlighting the contrast.

- Break down every step in the use of the rule and address each of them through practice.

- Use as many ways as you can think of to explain the rule. The more angles, analogies and visual representations you can use to explain the rule, the more likely it will stick. Try to come up with something memorable, like an acronym, a visual narrative or a diagram. But remember to keep the focus on practice.

- Plan your examples carefully, ensuring they are clear and unambiguous; don't improvise.

- Recycle the same vocabulary throughout the lesson in order to ease the cognitive load on students; the variety of tasks should keep the students interested.

- Make use of spaced learning and "interleaving" as far as possible. Research shows that items are better remembered when the exposure is spread out across time and mixed in with other language or activities.

Making the most of grammar worksheets

Some teachers dislike the idea of using worksheets, arguing that they're boring and often incorporate meaningless manipulation of language. I'd argue that excellent teachers know how to distinguish between a good worksheet and a bad one. They're also meticulous about choosing the right one for their class, not just the one provided with the text book. They use a worksheet for a specific purpose, most commonly to drill previously presented grammatical forms.

A worksheet either printed off for students or displayed on the board may initially seem a dull prospect for a lesson, but if we accept the old adage that "practice makes perfect" they're usually a necessary part of a language teacher's toolkit. Text book exercises and worksheets are often short of examples and don't allow enough opportunity for repetitive practice. How can we exploit worksheets to the best effect?

Practising past (preterite) tense

Imagine you are working with a sheet like the one in Box 7.1.

Box 7.1: Practising past (preterite) tense

1   We _____ the car to get to the station. (to take)
2   You _____ the tickets online. (to buy)
3   We _____ at the airport at 10.30. (to arrive)
4   You _____ in the departure lounge for half an hour. (to wait)
5   The plane _____ on time. (to take off)
6   During the flight I _____ a film. (to watch)

Add at least ten more examples

Consider the following points as an exercise in using your critical judgement about methodology when it comes to using worksheets.

1. Teacher-led approach

Read out a prompt from the list and get a student to answer, then get other individuals to repeat, then the whole class. This can be done with hands up or no hands up. Hands up allows you to choose quicker students as good role-models before weaker ones have a go.

Strengths. This approach is very old school, but highly effective for attentive classes, supplies lots of TL and allows you to pick out specific students. It's good for differentiating between students of different abilities and for providing listening practice. Class control is easier to manage and students hear good models, i.e. yours.

Weaknesses. It demands great attention from less attentive classes and only one student speaks at a time, except when there is choral repetition. You need to keep up a brisk pace or attention will quickly wane. Many students find answering in class embarrassing; does this kind of pressure aid language learning? Psychologists tell us we learn more effectively when we're relaxed.

2. Pair-work approach

After some whole-class practice as above, you can quickly move to pair work where one partner acts as teacher and the other as student, or the two students can alternate roles.

Strengths. Students get to speak and listen a lot in the TL and can support each other. There's little embarrassment factor because the pressure is off.

Weaknesses. Class control needs to be good so that students don't speak too much English or waste time. Perhaps insist on a "no English" rule. The disadvantage is that students may hear wrong answers and poor models of pronunciation, so they don't receive optimum input.

3. Student takes the lead and acts as teacher

After a brief demonstration, ask a volunteer, preferably a more able one, to step up and run the class.

Strengths. Similar to (1), though models may be less good. The class will listen extra hard and find the process amusing. The volunteer will learn teaching/leadership skills.

Weaknesses. As (1) in as far as each student may end up not saying much. The focus is more on listening, but that's not necessarily a bad thing.

4. Using mini-whiteboards

You can adapt approach (1) to involve more students actively by giving each student a mini-whiteboard and marker pen. As an answer is given all students must hold up their board with true/false or a mark indicating correct or wrong.

Strengths. As (1) plus more involvement from all the class.

Weaknesses. Largely as (1).

5. Combine skills

Use approach (1) but, as attention wanes, quickly go to oral prompts with written answers. Then get them to work quietly or in pairs doing written responses to written prompts.

Strengths. All students are actively engaged with listening to good models, reading and writing. This is good for behaviour management. You need to insist on silence.

Weaknesses. It's hard to check that all students are keeping up and writing accurate answers. There's little differentiation if the teacher controls the pace, i.e. when students are working alone there's more chance for going at their own pace and asking questions.

6. Give answers, students choose prompt

This is a simple variation which helps vary the lesson and provide a fresh angle for students. Let's say you've issued a sheet with 15 prompts (sentences, questions, etc.). Don't read the prompt, but give an answer and the students have to supply the correct prompt from the sheet. This can be done in pairs.

Strengths. This may be an easy way in to a worksheet. Students don't have to create a response, just read one already supplied. The focus is on comprehension rather than production.

Weaknesses. It's often easier therefore less challenging, since there's no need to show syntactic skill.

7. Supply alternative answers, students choose the best one

Again, this has the merit of making a worksheet more approachable for lower-attaining students. A student could read aloud a prompt, then the teacher supplies two answers (a) and (b). Students then vote for (a) or (b).

Strengths. Good for listening comprehension, the pressure is off and all are involved.

Weaknesses. Little production is needed, and there is a need to watch out for the peer effects if there is voting.

8. Get students to make up their own examples

Once a group seems to have mastered a point allow them to make up their own examples or even write their own worksheet.

Strengths. Allows students to be creative, show off their use of the new point and be amusing. This provides an excellent homework assignment. It allows students to compare work in the next lesson, try out their worksheet on a partner or the teacher, and reinforce the language acquired in the previous lesson.

Weaknesses. Nothing to speak of, but be sure that all students have mastered the point or it could end up being a disastrous homework!

Translation

Although the grammar-translation approach is largely discredited as a means of producing good listeners and fluent speakers, translation is often a part of assessment regimes and most teachers find it useful to incorporate elements of it in lessons. Generally speaking, the best teachers do translation (in both directions) in moderation, since using it excessively is bound to mean you'll supply less TL input to students and give them insufficient time to practise writing independently in the TL. You have to ask the question: "if I'm doing translation what am I not doing?" Translating into English at higher levels is partly about a student's skill in using English, although it does reveal detailed understanding of written or spoken texts. Translating into the TL can help to fix the accurate use of grammar, as we've seen above, and is useful where accuracy is a requirement of the syllabus.

Translating whole sentences or paragraphs into the TL is best done towards the end of a teaching sequence since it's a challenging, high-level skill requiring a solid foundation for success.

Here is a selection of ways of using translation into the TL in the classroom.

- **Teacher-led sessions.** Sentences or a passage are translated with hands up or no hands up. This is very traditional and has considerable merit. Students are subject to a high level of modelling and get to think like the teacher. The downside is that only one student talks at a time if you elicit answers and there's no guarantee that all students are paying attention. (Your job in this instance is to make certain they do!) To ensure students are involved, get them to write material down so that they're active and use whatever techniques you have up your sleeve to get all students thinking (deadly stares, eyebrows up, jokes, no hands up, asking individuals to repeat the previous answer, etc.) Make sure students get enough thinking time and that the quickest don't dominate. Notes can be taken in class, then written up at home.

- **Running translation.** Students work in pairs. Display in a few places around the classroom the passage or set of sentences to be translated. The "runner" finds the English or TL from the classroom wall and the scribe (maybe with the runner's help) translates. You can make this a race.

- **Find the translation.** Give students a list of quite hard sentences, short paragraphs or even individual words for beginners. Post or hide translations around the classroom for them to find individually or in teams. Make it competitive.

- **Google Translate.** Allow students to use this to see how well it does and to make corrections where they see fit. They'll learn something from the process and, let's face it, if they get the chance, many will use it anyway.

- **Gapped passages.** These can be produced in the TL, with phrases at the bottom in English to be translated and inserted where appropriate. This sort of scaffolded task has the added advantage of providing some TL input and a focus on meaning. It would suit lower-achieving classes.

- **Dictation-translation**. You just read sentences in English for students individually or in pairs to translate, perhaps using mini-whiteboards. The best answers could be rewarded. This would suit high-achieving groups.

- **Choose the best translation**. Give a paragraph in English with three TL versions of it. The students select the best one. You can make them as easy or hard as you want.

- **Parallel texts.** Use these in English and the TL to model effective translation.

- **Faulty translations** of sentences or a passage. Give these out for students to correct individually or in pairs. You could make it a race. They come up and show you their corrected versions.

- **Get excellent students to be the teacher** of a small group. They then play-act and model good answers. Class control needs to be tip-top for this, but it can be enjoyable and productive.

- **Show examples of badly translated signs**. These are amusing and easy to find online.

- **Use translation cue cards**. Put students into pairs and have them engage in conversations by getting them to translate their cues into the TL.

Explaining grammar rules

This is an important skill in itself and can, as we've seen, be done either before you practise a structure or after the structure has been practised, seen or heard in context. Explanations, as I've mentioned, are almost always best done in English for reasons of clarity. Keep explanations as short and simple as possible without sacrificing too much accuracy. Anticipating what students find hard takes experience and new teachers often overestimate what students understand. Explaining well means repeating and rephrasing as necessary, using visual aids, translation and metaphors to help students. This is where skilled use of presentational tools such as PowerPoint, Prezi or the interactive board can come into play. Make presentations as uncluttered and memorable as possible. If, with very able classes, you're talking about grammar in the TL it's useful to make sure students know TL terms such as *noun, verb, tense, subject, object* and so on.

Some grammatical rules are so complicated that it's not worth trying to teach them. For example, trying to get across the subtle difference between the immediate future ("going to") and the simple future tense ("shall/will") isn't worth dwelling on too long. Your syllabus may well dictate what structures you should be teaching, but even in this case you need to exercise judgement according to your class's abilities. Don't feel you have to cover every detail of the syllabus; time limitations may make this impossible anyway.

As we've seen above, it's useful to compare and contrast the TL rule with its English equivalent, e.g. when explaining the concept of imperfect and past preterite (perfect) tenses, many students find it easier to think of "was doing/used to do" versus "did", even if direct translations are not precise equivalents. You have to weigh up clarity against total accuracy. When working on the present tense you're bound to mention the three forms of the present in English (*I play, I'm playing, I do play*). This can lead to interesting discussions and raise students' curiosity about grammar in general.

You'll also find that after explanation and frequent practice, some structures just don't seem to stick. This can be frustrating, but at this point you just need to move on; perhaps the students aren't ready to acquire that area of grammar just yet. Perhaps your teaching will bear fruit at a later stage.

Is there another way?

Research and experience strongly suggest that in many cases our best attempts to get students to become fluent, independent users of grammar are doomed to failure. There just isn't enough class time. In addition, there's plenty of research evidence to show that students acquire structures in their own order, which often doesn't correspond with the order we teach them. Some conclude from this that it's futile to teach grammar at all and that we should simply expose students to meaningful messages, letting the processes of natural acquisition take their course. We acquire grammar naturally in our first language, so why not adopt the same approach in second-language teaching?

I'd argue against this approach in school settings for a number of reasons:

- There isn't enough time in lessons for students to pick up grammar just by exposure to TL input – much more input is required.

- Incorporating explicit grammar teaching and practice does seem to help at least some students become proficient.

- Students usually value explanations and the chance to practise.

- Some students enjoy studying grammar for its own sake.

- The predominant view of research scholars favours a combination of TL input and some focus on grammatical form.

- Knowing formal grammatical rules helps students monitor the accuracy of their speech and writing.

- While we can't know for sure how students acquire grammar, it remains possible that grammatical skill can be developed through explanation, practice and "internalisation" (automatisation) of rules.

Box 7.2: Tech tips

Use interactive grammar websites such as **Languages Online**, **Language Gym** and the text manipulation program **Textivate** to work on grammatical structures. Textivate lets you author your own exercises.

The app **Duolingo** is, in 2017, the most widely used in the world. It involves using grammar to translate sentences and put words in the correct order to make grammatical sentences. With **Duolingo Clubs**, users can gather into social clubs to keep track of each other's learning. There are weekly leaderboards and users can leave comments on their friends' progress.

Make skilled use of the **interactive whiteboard (IWB)** to present, model and practise grammar, e.g. highlighting and creating instant gaps, using the iris and curtain functions. Most courses are published with online interactive material.

Boardworks is a commercial program with elaborate units of work designed for the IWB. It can be a very useful add-on to your main course.

Triptico is a website and downloadable IWB tool with a range of apps you can use to enhance grammar learning. The Word Magnets tool within Triptico allows you to move colour-coded words around on an interactive board to form grammatical sentences, for example.

Explain Everything is a popular and extremely flexible IWB app that allows you to make attractive videos by importing and annotating pictures and audio. The videos could be used as part of a **flipped learning** model, whereby students study the grammar point at home first before it's practised in class. Explain Everything has other uses, e.g. if a class has not done their homework very well you can take a photo of a piece of work, import it into the app, then annotate it using the pen, pointer and highlighter tools. This can be done "live" on the board or saved on to a virtual learning environment.

ShowMe turns an iPad into an IWB and also allows you to record voice-over whiteboard tutorials.

YouTube. For French, **Maud Sullivan** has created 57 grammar presentation videos which could be used for flipped learning. They're all delivered in French and would suit good intermediate and advanced students. I don't particularly recommend this model in general since I believe it's better for the class teacher to explain points, but it could make for an interesting variation to your normal practice. Try **Señor Jordan**'s videos for Spanish – he has an engaging style, mixing English with Spanish. **Easy Languages** is worth checking out for German videos featuring young Germans demonstrating grammar in action with subtitled translations in English.

Concluding remarks

There's been heated debate among academics for many years about how useful it is to teach grammar. We've seen that some argue that a teacher's time is better spent just focusing on meaningful input. The general consensus, however, is that it's useful to teach some rules and practise structures, as long as you don't do it too much or reach the point of boring students.

How much grammar you do may well depend on the class you're teaching, your goals for that class and the type of assessment they'll undergo. The more meaningful and enjoyable you can make grammar, the better. If you teach it with great skill you should be able to create enough interest to be successful. Many students enjoy the cognitive, puzzle-solving aspect of grammar and translation. There's something almost tangible about *knowing rules* which students often value. They learn rules and concepts in other subjects, so might expect it in their language lessons too. Mastering a point provides a sense of achievement in a subject where it's relatively hard to produce short-term gains. So grammar has its place, but in the next chapter I'll look at something even more important.

Chapter 8

Words and chunks

Introduction

What stops students speaking and understanding, is it poor grammar or a lack of words? Perhaps for too long we've favoured grammar over the words and phrases that convey most of the meaning in what we say. This chapter will examine the learning of vocabulary, emphasising that this is much more than just picking up words through exposure. Although acquiring vocabulary in meaningful contexts is still the main way to recycle and embed it in students' memories, there are many tricks you can employ to enhance memory and exploit those vocabulary lists we find in text books. The best teachers are able to make words memorable. How do they do this?

Teach lots of words!

When I began teaching I believed students would pick up vocabulary as they went along and that it was best to both speak and listen to lots of TL and practise the grammar. Over the years I came to believe that teaching words was the most important thing you can do. If your students can recognise and quickly retrieve from memory a few hundred words they'll be able to cope well with very basic conversation on a range of simple situations up to intermediate level.

For words to be remembered, students need to see or hear them numerous times over a significant length of time. Words should preferably be seen or heard within longer chunks so that students get used to recognising word boundaries in the stream of sound. If you keep that in mind, you can see where the effort needs to lie. It's about providing as many different ways as possible for students to encounter high-frequency contextualised words and chunks in the limited time you have available.

Note that I say both words and chunks. Why? If we take the example of nouns, which have gender in French, German and Spanish, if students regularly hear the nouns together with an article (i.e. as two-word chunks) they're more likely to instantly recall the gender. This is how children pick up gender in their native tongue. So, when presenting lists of nouns to be learned, it makes more sense to learn them with an article (preferably the one they're most commonly accompanied by) rather than followed by the gender (*m, f, n*) in brackets.

Other chunks include formulaic expressions (*how are you?*), idioms (*he drinks like a fish*), or phrasal expressions of various sorts. These need to be memorised as chunks for instant retrieval. Even the phrase *I don't understand* is a chunk. My experience is that students are able to incorporate memorised chunks into unrehearsed speech.

Teach patterns

A useful way to enable students to recognise words and to understand and accurately produce words they've never come across is to point out similar patterns across the TL and English. Advanced students develop an instinctive sense for these, but you can accelerate the process. Look at the selection of patterns in Tables 8.1, 8.2 and 8.3. These are worth spelling out to students.

Table 8.1 Spanish lexical patterns compared with English

Pattern	Examples
The Spanish word adds an *–o* (and sometimes an accent) or changes a final '–e' in English to an *–o* in Spanish.	aspecto, automático, económico, activo.
The Spanish word adds an *–a* (and sometimes an accent) to the English word.	lista, idiota.
Words ending in '–ist' in English often end in *–ista* in Spanish.	pianista, comunista.
Spanish changes a final '–e' to an *–a*.	medicina.
The Spanish word adds an *–e*.	aire, arte.
Words which end in *–ía* or *–ia* in Spanish and '–y' in English.	biología, economía, tragedia.
Verbs which end with *–ar* in the infinitive in Spanish and with '–e' in English.	admirar, confirmar, reservar, server.

Words and chunks

Table 8.2 French lexical patterns compared with English

Pattern	Examples
Words which end with –e or –é in French and with '–y' in English.	*beauté, liberté, mystère, armée.*
Words which end with –aire in French and with '–ar' or '–ary' in English.	*secondaire, primaire, solaire.*
Words which end with –el in French and with '–al' in English.	*individuel, officiel, naturel, formel.*
Verbs which end with –er in French and with '–ate' in English.	*assassiner, cultiver, décorer, activer.*
Words which end with –e in French and '–a' in English.	*drame, propagande.*
Words which end with –eur in French and with '–our', '–or' or '-er' in English.	*acteur, empereur, vigueur, sauveur.*

Table 8.3 German spellings compared with English

Pattern	Examples
Words where –ch in German is replaced by '–k' in English.	*Koch, Machen.*
Words where –t in German is replaced by '–d' in English.	*trinken, Tropfen, Tochter.*
Words where –d in German is replaced by '–th' in English.	*das, denken, drei, Ding.*
Words where –ss in German is replaced by '–t' in English.	*Wasser, hasse.*
Words where –cht in German is replaced by '–ght' in English.	*Nacht, Flucht.*
Words where –z in German is replaced by '–t' in English.	*Zunge, zehn, zwei, zwanzig.*
Words where –v in German is replaced by '–f' in English.	*Vater, Volk, vier.*

Make words memorable

Research suggests that when you first introduce a new word you should do so repeatedly. Retention is also aided when a word is learned and practised in memorable contexts. To do this you can use striking pictures and objects, associate words with their English equivalent, use rhymes, tunes, mimes and gestures. You can associate words with a memorable experience (a visit, funny moment in the classroom), for example, make something, play a game, perform a sketch, say the words aloud, practise hearing and seeing them at the same time, use a vocabulary learning app and, above all, **repeat** them over time.

Studies also show that most students forget a word within a week if they learn it just once. When students encounter a new word they're more likely to remember it if they see the spelling at the same time. This is an argument for using flashcards with the written word included. The impact a word makes on the student when it's first learned plays a significant role in how well it will be remembered.

To enable words to be recycled you need to include them as often as possible in your interactions with the class (another justification for using lots of TL), use them in listening and reading texts and get students to learn them from lists. Vocabulary learning at home is a habit you can usually train students into, making sure they know how they'll be tested and, for example, what their pass mark will be. Teachers often use apps for this purpose. If you prefer students to do other tasks at home (perhaps because they don't do homework reliably), you can do short instant-recall vocabulary tests in class: "You've got five minutes to memorise these 15 words, then I'll give you a test from Spanish to English." Then: "Now you have another 5 minutes, after which I'll test them from English into Spanish." If you administer vocabulary tests you can adjust their level of challenge by providing gapped words, doing half from TL to English, half from English to TL, or giving the first letter(s) of each word. Make sure students know that their work will lead to success and longer-term retention.

It's important to note that vocabulary quizzes can become a successful habit for students. Once they achieve success they're more likely to want to maintain their standard. Some students are competitive about their marks and take great pride in scoring highly.

Below are some other means by which words can be made more memorable for students.

Phonological hooks

Students can write down words in the form of a mind map, associating them with as many words starting or ending with the same sounds. These don't necessarily have to be TL words. This technique can be enhanced by creating sentences using rhyming words, e.g. if the target word is "fair" – "my hair is fair" or "hired" – "he was hired then fired". This is based on the principle that words stored in the brain are more closely connected to others with which they alliterate, chime and rhyme.

Emotional associations

Associate new words with people or objects that are meaningful for students. So, for instance, when learning physical or personality adjectives, use them to describe people that mean a lot to the class, possibly by virtue of those very attributes, e.g. "Albert Einstein was smart" or "Usain Bolt is fast". The effectiveness of this technique is based on the principle that an emotional investment in learning information increases its distinctiveness and consequently the chances of its retention.

Categorising by meaning

Give students the task of sorting words into different categories based on their meaning.

Example: you are trying to teach the words *argumentative, noisy, talkative, ill, lazy, active, sociable, smart, hard-working, modest, cheerful, amusing, talkative, slim, beautiful, bad-tempered, faithful, annoying, fit, affluent, depressed, underprivileged, frustrated* and *vindictive.*

First ask students to simply divide them into two categories: positive and negative; secondly, into physical appearance, personality and emotional states and thirdly, you may want to narrow it down further still. The reason why this approach works is because it requires "cognitive investment", i.e. it creates connections between the words while at the same time involving creativity, all of which results in deeper processing and better retention of the words.

Categorising by word class (part of speech)

When you have a mix of nouns, adjectives, verbs, prepositions and so on, a further type of classification you can use is by grammatical word class. Research suggests that words belonging to the same class are more strongly linked in the brain. In addition, when we try to understand input through listening and reading we use our knowledge of grammar to analyse it.

Word association

This familiar filler activity actually helps reinforce memory as students make links across the various semantic fields in their brains. For any new word to be learned, think of others that spring to mind and work through chains of words.

Narrow reading to recycle words and chunks

A useful task type to encourage the recycling of vocabulary is narrow reading or narrow listening (mentioned in Chapter 7) whereby students read or hear a set of about four to six short texts, all on a similar theme and sharing some of the same vocabulary and structures. By doing a series of exercises on the paragraphs, students get to hear and use items over and over. Accompanying tasks can include true/false/not mentioned, gap-filling, matching starts and ends of sentences, TL questions and translation. In Box 8.1 is a set of four French paragraphs which could be read or listened to. I've highlighted in bold type where there are common words or chunks. The speakers/writers are talking about recent holidays.

Box 8.1: Mes vacances récentes

Depuis longtemps, je voulais visiter Goa et finalement, **l'année dernière**, j'y suis allée avec mes amis. **On a logé** dans un Air B & B **pendant** huit jours parce qu'on n'avait pas beaucoup d'argent. **Du coup** on a toujours cherché des **endroits** pas chers pour manger. **Quel soleil! On a visité** des lieux touristiques comme la cathédrale, les marchés locaux et aussi les boîtes de nuit célèbres. J'ai goûté des fruits de mer et des poissons de types **différents. On a fait** du rafting et du surf à la mer. Mais **le meilleur moment** pour moi était le jour où **on a fait une promenade** épuisante. **L'année prochaine je ferai un petit job**, **ça me permettra** d'économiser pour mes vacances. (Laurence)

L'année dernière on a passé des vacances extraordinaires en Californie. **Je voulais** y aller **depuis longtemps. On a loué** une voiture **pendant** quinze jours. Impossible de tout raconter, mais **le meilleur moment** était **la promenade** en Segway à San

---

Francisco. Los Angeles était bien, mais **il y avait trop de circulation** sur les routes. J'ai adoré le parc naturel de Yosemite, avec ses beaux paysages, ses énormes arbres et **panoramas si spectaculaires. Chaque** soir **on a logé** dans un hôtel **différent**. Je n'ai pas trop apprécié la cuisine américaine, mais mon frère a dit qu'il mangerait volontiers des hamburgers **tous les jours. L'année prochaine je ferai un petit job** pour économiser pour un **voyage** en Espagne avec mes copains. (Didier)

L'année dernière j'ai passé mes vacances d'été avec ma famille dans le midi de la France. On y va depuis longtemps. On a logé dans un vieux gîte au centre du village de La Palme près de la Méditerranée. Nous sommes partis sur le ferry de Portsmouth le jeudi soir et on est arrivés à notre destination tard le samedi soir. Le **voyage** était **épuisant** parce qu'**il y avait trop de circulation** et il pleuvait tout le temps. Le jour **on a visité** plusieurs **endroits** historiques car je m'intéresse aux autres cultures. Un jour, **on a fait une promenade** dans le petit train dans un parc naturel dans les Pyrénées. Les paysages **étaient** très calmes et **les panoramas étaient si spectaculaires** que j'ai pu prendre beaucoup de jolies photos. (Thierry)

Chaque année au mois de février ma famille et moi, on va dans les Alpes faire du ski. Cette fois **on a loué** un chalet près de Morzine. **Quelle neige! Du coup** on a pu skier presque **tous les jours**. C'est amusant, mais très **épuisant** aussi. Le soir on a mangé au chalet ensemble ou, des fois, on est allés au restaurant dans le village manger de la fondue, par exemple. **L'année prochaine** je voudrais faire des cours de snowboard. Pour **faire des économies je ferai un petit job** au centre de jardinage près de chez nous ; **ça me permettra** d'acheter du matériel de ski. (Cécile)

Vocabulary games

I have to recommend the book *Fun Learning Activities for Modern Foreign Languages* (2015) in which Jake Hunton presents a wide range of games and game-like activities, many of which have the aim of embedding vocabulary knowledge. Just to give you one example for near-beginners: in the game "Bob-Up Classic" Jake shows a PowerPoint slide with 13 TL sentences relating to personal descriptions, e.g. in French *J'ai les cheveux blonds; J'ai les yeux verts.* The class is divided in two with each half having a captain (who gets to wear a football captain's armband). The captain distributes cards with numbers on them, 1–13, one to each student on each team. You call out a number at random and whoever has that number on each team has to "bob up" and say the phrase in TL then translate it into English. The quickest student wins a point for the team. Jake stresses that this is not a frivolous game and that it helps with retrieval of previously learned language beyond the single word level.

Other activities from Jake's treasure trove of ideas include Vocab Piler, where students write down six of their favourite words in the TL and in English. Then over the next five to ten minutes they go round the room and listen to other students' six words, writing down any new ones they hear.

Making the most of vocabulary lists

Text books often contain lists of words or phrases to be set to memory. There are many ways you might choose to exploit these. Below is a selection from a list in The Language Teacher Toolkit (Smith and Conti, 2016 – see bibliography).

1) Get students to **cover the words and test** themselves, or get someone else to test them.

2) Use a **word fan**. Students make a fan (folding the paper several times) and write the English word on one side, TL word on the other. This may appeal to younger students who could use it for reference.

3) Students **concentrate on the most difficult words**, linking them to something they know, e.g. clay keys (the French word for key is *clé* – pronounced like clay).

4) Students **write the words out** over and over – English with TL and vice versa – doing more and more from memory each time.

5) Students **make up a rhythm**, tapping out the words as they say them.

6) Students **record the words** on their mobile device and listen back, e.g. on the way to school.

7) Students **sort the words** by gender/groups/patterns, e.g. fruit/vegetables or colour code them.

8) Students **group the words alphabetically**.

9) Suggest students **write the words on Post-it notes** and stick them up around their bedrooms.

10) **You write out the words with letters missing**, e.g. vowels, then get students to do gap-fill.

11) **Design a word search** for students with the TL words in.

12) Have students play a **paired game**. Each person gives a word they've learned; the first one unable to give a word loses.

13) Students play a **mime game** in pairs. Each partner does a mime and the other has to guess the word.

14) Play **"running reporter"**: a vocabulary list is put somewhere far away (e.g. at the back of the class). In teams of two, one student goes to the list and tries to memorise as many words as accurately as they can, then returns to their partner who acts as scribe. The first pair to complete the list accurately wins.

15) **Read aloud a vocabulary list** to the class. Students repeat. It seems obvious, but speaking words aloud can help fix them in students' minds. You can make this more fun (and improve students' pronunciation) by whispering, raising the voice, creating a rhythm or even singing. Pull faces, getting the class to watch your lips.

16) Get students to **cover up the TL words**. You then supply the first syllable or sound of a word and they have to complete it with the rest of the word. This can be amusing. You can do the same but supply the last sound or syllable of the word.

17) Give **oral definitions** of words. Students write down the answers. This is harder, suits very able groups, but provides good listening practice. It's very easy to tailor to your particular class.

18) **Use synonyms and antonyms** to elicit words.

19) **Do "aural anagrams"**. Spell out words with the letters jumbled up. The students guess the word as fast as they can. You can make this a team or paired game.

20) Make up a **code-breaking** task for the class. Do this in the form of a worksheet. You can use numbers or symbols from your computer such as Wingdings.

21) Makevoneoenormouscwordafrombtheulistlyouahaversetytheclass. Place added letters between the words. These could spell out another word or phrase.

22) Play **strip bingo**. This involves giving each students a strip of paper (e.g. a sheet of A4 cut vertically in two). The students write out about ten words they've been learning from a vocabulary list top to bottom on the strip. You read aloud words from the word list in random order. Each time the student hears a word at the top or bottom of their list they tear it off. The winner is the student who gets rid of all their words. You have to make sure you read aloud

the same words on several occasions for this to work effectively. Needless to say, students get to hear words repeatedly which aids memory retention.

23) Play **word bingo**. This works in the same way as traditional bingo, but students write down words from a list instead of numbers.

24) Students play a **dominoes** game – make up dominoes with words and their definitions in English or TL or translations. Each domino will have a word at one end and either a definition or meaning in English at the other. This might be recommended for lower-attaining classes.

25) **Collocations:** you produce pairs of related words, cut them up and students have to put the words together.

26) **Running-to-the-board** games. Write up words on the board in a random pattern. Create two teams; give each student a number so each team has a person with the same number. Give a definition or translation and call out a number. The first student to rush to the board and touch the word gets a point. Some teachers let students use a fly swat to add a greater element of fun. Alternatively, get two students to stand by the board and do the same activity. Change pairs every few minutes.

27) Play a **spot the difference** game. Display two pictures and ask students to identify differences. You can either display the pictures together, or one after the other as a test of memory. This task simultaneously allows you to practise negation.

Box 8.2: Tech tips

Apps come into their own in the area of vocabulary. Students who enjoy setting words to memory from their phone or tablet can use, at the time of writing, apps such as **Memrise, Brainscape, Vocab Express, Duolingo, Kahoot, StudyStack, Cramit, Quizizz** and **Quizlet**, for example.

Memrise is a community-driven flashcard site with interesting features, e.g. it supports audio, images and mnemonics. You don't just learn words, they say, but rather "plant" and "grow" them. You begin with seeing the word for the first time, and then the app cycles between multiple-choice flashcards with English – TL, TL – English and typing out the word in TL.

Brainscape has its own "Confidence-Based Repetition" system, i.e. you spend more time learning the things that you find challenging and less time on those you've already learned. With every flashcard, you're asked to gauge the difficulty level and decide how often you want to review that card. The adaptive learning algorithm then does its job of scheduling the card to come up at the best moment.

Duolingo provides written lessons and dictation, with speaking practice for more advanced students. It has games at different levels through which users can progress and a vocabulary section where learned words can be practised. Users gain "experience points" as they learn a language, e.g. when they complete a lesson. Skills are considered "learned" when a student completes all the lessons associated with the skill. You win one point for each correct answer, lose one for each error, and validate the lesson when you reach ten points. As the goal of Duolingo is to get people to learn the language, each skill (containing between one and ten lessons) has a "strength bar" that corresponds to the computer's estimate of how strongly certain words or constructions still exist in the learner's memory. After a certain duration of time, strength bars fade, indicating the need for a user to refresh or re-study that lesson, or to strengthen weak skills. Courses can teach upwards of 2,000 words. Duolingo is a handy option for students who may have finished other tasks.

Vocab Express has many users in UK schools. It's a paid-for app for schools and individuals that helps students learn vocabulary and grammar. There is pre-loaded and categorised vocabulary from all major English and Welsh examination boards as well as textbook publishers. Students are motivated through a system of scoreboards, monitored by the teacher through a comprehensive set of real-time tracking tools. It can be used for homework, in-class activities or for cover lessons with minimal preparation.

Quizlet allows you to customise sets of vocabulary for you to focus on. These can then be studied in different modes which involve game elements, e.g., in Gravity Mode, definitions scroll vertically down the screen in the shape of asteroids. You type the term that goes with the definition before it reaches the bottom of the screen. **Quizlet Live** can be used to pit teams or individuals against each other. There are many ready-made Quizlet activities to be found online without having to use the app.

Lingua.ly lets students look up and save words they come across when reading online articles, then recommends relevant texts for them to read in order to extend vocabulary and improve their reading skills. Students can click on any word and, after showing a definition and playing an audio version of the word, the system stores it in the student's personal inbox. These words can then be practised and repeated with activities that ask students to match the words with their translations.

One issue with all these programs is that they often focus on isolated words (although Duolingo most certainly doesn't – it relies strongly on translations of sentences). This means that most of them do not feature much, if any, communication or exposure to longer chunks of language, but they certainly appeal to many students and teachers who often choose to use them for homework tasks.

Concluding remarks

It's virtually impossible to learn a vocabulary item from a single encounter. From one study it's been estimated that students need to see or hear a word between ten and 16 times for it to stick. Coming across words incidentally over time will play a major role in students picking them up, but to be most effective you need to make sure you provide opportunities for repeated encounters with words and chunks. The more you can space out these encounters the better, as research shows learning usually occurs best when you distribute it over time, with spaces in between each learning opportunity.

Some teachers frown upon using translation to explain the meaning of new words. I'd argue that where explanation can be easily done in the TL, you should do so, since you're providing more input for students, but if this gets laborious or causes confusion and subsequent loss of concentration, then a translation in English is fine and, what's more, it satisfies the student's natural desire to know "how do we say this in English?".

Chapter 9

Dissecting a lesson: speaking

Introduction

In this chapter I'll consider how effective teachers develop spoken proficiency with their classes. Research in the field of second language acquisition strongly suggests the best way to help students progress in all the skills is by providing as much interesting spoken and written input as possible, along with opportunities for spoken interaction. How do we help students become independent speakers who can go beyond memorised utterances?

Firstly, let's be clear: there are no silver bullets! If your time is limited to, say, 400 classroom hours plus homework in 5 years, there may be a limit to what can be achieved. The majority of students will only be able to use a limited repertoire of mainly pre-learned, rehearsed language, perhaps with a little ability to improvise. If the students are fortunate enough to be taught by excellent teachers for several years a larger number will achieve genuine independence. A minority will become surprisingly proficient speakers within a limited range, especially if they get a full immersion experience such as an exchange visit. This is the icing on the cake.

So your job is to provide as much comprehensible TL as possible, moving from easier to harder language, explaining and practising a selection of grammar along the journey, recycling vocabulary and structures as much as possible. You can say to classes: "If you listen hard, read carefully, have a go and do your work, nature will take its course." For able students nature takes its course much more quickly.

In Chapter 13 I list a wide range of oral interactions you can generate in the classroom, all of which produce input and talk. Here, I'm going to look at three specific lessons for **intermediate** and **advanced** students and how they combine both TL input and opportunities for spontaneous speech. I'll also suggest a few ways to encourage spontaneous talk.

Lesson sequence 1: from comprehension to talk

Exploiting a fairy tale

The source text here is a simplified version of the fairy tale Cinderella, written for **intermediate** students. You can translate it into the language you teach. Fairy tales are a great source of comprehensible input since students usually know the story already and enjoy the content. (We'll ignore any questionable moral messages the text might convey – these could be a good subject for a separate discussion!)

Box 9.1: Cinderella

There was once a beautiful girl, an orphan, who lived in a big house with her father. Her stepmother had two daughters who were ugly and unkind. The stepmother and the two sisters forced Cinderella to do all the housework every day. She had to do the laundry, wash the dishes, do the ironing and prepare all the meals. Each day she also had to remove the ashes from the fireplace. This is why she was called Cinderella.

One day the prince of the kingdom organised a ball because he wanted to find a bride. All the girls in the realm were invited. Cinderella's two step-sisters, helped by their mother, made all the preparations for the ball. Cinderella was not allowed to go to the ball. She was sad not to be going but did not dare ask permission to go. She cried so much that her fairy godmother heard her and suddenly appeared. The fairy used her magic to turn Cinderella into a beautiful woman. She created an amazing dress, slippers made of glass and a coach and horses.

So Cinderella could go to the ball, but she had to promise to return before midnight. When she arrived at the ball everyone was amazed by her beauty. The prince invited her to dance. At the end of the evening she was so happy that she forgot the time. In her haste, she lost a glass slipper. The prince was determined to find his loved one, so he went to visit all the girls in the kingdom and asked them to try on the slipper. He promised to marry the girl who was able to wear the shoe.

When he arrived at Cinderella's house, the step-sisters tried on the slipper, but it didn't fit. Then he asked Cinderella to try on the slipper. The prince was amazed to discover that poor Cinderella was the girl he had met.

They soon married and lived happily ever after.

Table 9.1 A lesson sequence: from comprehension to talk

Teacher	Students	Commentary
Pre-reading: display some key words on the board (*prince, king, shoe, glass, housework, step-sister, ball, coach and horses*). Ask students to guess what they are going to be working on.	Students listen and then work out what they are going to be talking about. Easy!	This immediately raises interest and provides some key vocabulary which students will hear, read and use later. Any unfamiliar words which are not clear cognates (depending on the language) can be explained by definition, gesture or translation.
Display and/or hand out the story to be read. Read it to them.	Students follow the text. A class with poor literacy might be asked to follow with a ruler beneath each line.	Scan the class now and again to check students are following.
Ask students to read aloud short sections of the text. Make any corrections to pronunciation. Make sure any reader repeats a mispronounced word. Correct sympathetically.	Hands up or no hands up for this. Individuals read short sections.	You could use whole group reading aloud if the class is well trained in this. This keeps everyone involved. You could use this opportunity to focus on intonation, an often neglected area in language lessons. Teach the class any patterns you know, e.g. the rising intonation and slight phrase-end stress in French.
Make false statements for the class to correct. You can make these as silly as you want to hold interest: *The fairy godmother created a Ferrari*.	Hands up, with occasional teacher choice of student. Students can essentially reread sections of text to do this activity.	At times like this you need to be really vigilant about who is listening carefully. Use eye contact, choose any student who appears to be inattentive. Keep the whole class on the ball.
Now tell the class you're going to give them true/false/not mentioned statements. You can make these as subtle or as outrageous as you want, depending on the class.	Hands up or no hands up.	This tests your skill at judging precisely what you think the class can do. Pitching this sort of task accurately is vital.

Ask TL questions on the text.	Hands up or no hands up.	This demands more from the class as they have to decode the question, then use a different structure to answer. Even so, they can still lift from the text. Note how much recycling of language is already taking place.
Get students into pairs. Tell them that each partner has to make up true/false/not mentioned statements of their own. Give a time limit to add a sense of urgency.	Students work in pairs alternately testing their partner.	By now there has been enough input for students to talk, but they'll still be lifting from the text to a large degree.
Tell students to hide their text or just hide your displayed text. Get students, in pairs, to make as many statements as they can about the story in TL. Tell them that the first partner who can't say something is the loser. Tell them not to worry about making mistakes.	Students make up statements from memory. Some will no doubt improvise a bit at this point.	Monitor the pair work carefully. Accept hardly any chatting in English. Warn them specifically about this if necessary.
If the class still has enough energy, tell them each partner has to try to tell the story to the other. The partner must listen and make any corrections as they see fit.	More pair work. Students produce longer stretches of speech, mixing remembered language and improvising a bit more.	If this part is beyond your class, you can provide a gapped summary on the board for students to refer to. Make this as easy or as hard as it needs to be. You'll know in advance what your class's capabilities are likely to be.

See Table 9.1 for this sequence described in detail. Let me make it clear that it's one of many you could use, but I've ensured a logical progression, moving from easy to harder, input to output. It's this type of work, done many times over, that helps lead to longer-term proficiency. The same principle also works with lower level classes with easier texts. The sequence can be reinforced by adding further oral or written elements in the following lesson, e.g. an interview with Cinderella or a step-sister, or the story told from Cinderella's or the prince's point of view. High-attaining classes could be asked to write their own mini fairy tale, after having a TL discussion about the typical elements of the genre: good triumphing over evil, magic, moral messages and a happy ending.

Lesson sequence 2: from grammar to talk

Palmistry

In this section let's look at how we can move from teaching and practising a grammatical structure to more open-ended, semi-rehearsed oral exchanges with low-intermediate students. The lesson is based on using the future tense while playing palm reading. Before the sequence takes place it's assumed that students have been introduced to the future tense and had the chance to do some tasks to consolidate its use. This could be done, for instance, by reading and exploiting simple written and oral texts featuring the future tense, and doing oral work based on pairs of pictures such as those used in Chapter 7 – when we saw how the imperfect tense could be introduced or by doing interactive online grammar practice. **Table 9.2** shows this sequence in detail while **Table 9.3** indicates some possible displayed prompts.

Table 9.2 Palm reading

Activity	Commentary
Once you've spent a few lessons working on the future tense in various ways, explain that in this lesson you're going to get students to try out some palmistry. Explain what palmistry is and display a picture of a palm with the various lines marked.	Students should be interested to learn that palm reading (also known as palmistry or chiromancy) is a superstitious practice found in various countries around the world, with cultural variations. This pre-task introduction should raise interest.
Display a set of prompts in the future tense, using the second person singular form of the verb. See Table 9.3. Provide translations to the right of each prompt if you think the class needs them.	You may wish to go through the displayed prompts, reading them aloud and getting the class to repeat chorally. If a reminder is needed about the tense being used to link with previous work, then give it.

Activity	Commentary
Invite a student to come to the front and proceed to give them a palm reading, using a selection of language displayed. Adjust the level of difficulty to the class's level.	Bringing up a student will focus the class's attention effectively. Personalise the statements as much as possible.
Pair up students and tell them they're going to read each other's palms. Leave the prompts displayed and provide a handout copy. Scaffold the prompts as much as the class requires. Give plenty of examples of verbs to higher-attaining classes. Tell the students they have three minutes to read each other's palm.	Monitor the activity, ensuring the students remain in TL. Help out, gently correcting where needed.
Next, display some examples of questions which the student whose palm is being read can ask. See Table 9.3 again. These will be in the first person. Practise them through choral repetition.	Get the students to notice the different verb ending or form (depending on the language being taught).
Pair up students once more. This time they have to produce a conversation involving both future predictions and questions, e.g. *You will have lots of children – How many children will I have? – You will have four children.* Model a conversation yourself to make the task clear. Tell them they will have five minutes.	Monitor the activity, correcting where necessary and answering questions. Encourage the students to use what they know as far as possible; they can keep referring to their prompts on the handout.
Ask for volunteers to model their dialogue.	This provides a break in the lesson and a chance to hear good models. Hopefully the students will bring some humour to bear.
Elicit from the class, with hands up or no hands up, statements in the third person about partners' future lives. Recast answers as necessary, making third-person verb forms clear.	This is another chance for students to hear you model good verb forms. You can elicit further detail by asking more TL questions, depending on what students say. Use humour. Suggest absurd predictions.
Tell students that their written task will be to write some sentences, a paragraph or short essay on their own future lives. They should try to recycle the language they've used in class as far as possible. If they have few ideas about their future, suggest they make up an imaginary future, being as imaginative and /or humorous as possible. Give a minimum word length.	Tell students: "Use what you know". You can give more leeway to high-achieving classes. A minimum word length ensures you get a decent amount of work from each student. But tell stronger classes that you'll give bonus marks or look more favourably on work that shows greater length or originality.

Table 9.3 Palm-reading task prompts for display

• *You will have*	• *children, an English woman, a French husband*
• *You will be*	• *an American partner, a Spanish partner*
• *You will work*	• *in France, in England, in the USA, in Canada, in Australia, in Spain, in Germany*
• *You will live*	
• *You will play*	• *in an office, in a factory, in a school, on a farm, in a hospital*
• *You will do*	
• *You will go*	• *football, swimming, gymnastics, tennis, judo*
• *You will marry*	• *vegetarian*
• *You will like*	• *to the gym*
	• *in a big house, in a small apartment*
(With optional translations in English – extend if needed for higher-achieving classes.)	• *pilot, teacher, doctor, taxi driver, astronaut, journalist*
	• *wealthy, poor*
	• *TV, going to the cinema, theatre, reading, walking, sky-diving, music*

• *How many children will I have?*	• *Will I be married?*
• *Will I live in Germany?*	• *Which countries will I visit?*
• *Will I go to university?*	• *Where will I work?*
• *What will I study?*	• *What other pastimes will I have?*
• *Will I have any pets?*	• *What type of clothes will I wear?*
• *Will I win the lottery?*	• *Will I play a musical instrument?*

Lesson sequence 3: talking about the internet and social media

After six or seven years of language lessons with high-quality teaching, motivated students are nearly always able to use the TL spontaneously, some with remarkable skill given how relatively little time they've had to learn compared with native speakers. They don't come close to native speaker speed, range and use of idiom, but to all intents and purposes they're reasonably proficient. This opens up a huge range of possibilities for practising spontaneous TL use: working with texts, films, literature, video and doing general discussion of topical events or controversial issues. This can be a real joy when you see the fruits of both your work and theirs.

Table 9.4 presents one approach to developing further fluency on a typical advanced level topic: **the internet and social media**. This type of work would make great sense before you tackle a listening or reading text on the same topic.

Table 9.4 Developing advanced-level speaking

Teacher	Students	Commentary
Provide a lengthy TL bilingual vocabulary list of terms associated with the internet and social media. Include at least 50 words. Tell students to scan the list and that you will be asking them some questions in a few minutes.	Students read.	This just gives a moment for students to process the language, see what they know already, guess cognates and identify unknown words. This shows them why looking at the words is useful since it provides a focus and slight sense of urgency.
Give TL definitions of words. These could be synonyms, antonyms or longer definitions. Do about 20; judge the mood of the class to see how far you can go.	Students choose a word from the list. Hands up.	Longer definitions have the advantage of providing more input, demanding greater cognitive challenge in the process. Adjust the difficulty of your definitions to the class. Mix up easier and harder ones to differentiate between students.
Get students to repeat the same task in pairs, with partners taking turns to play the teacher role.	This allows students to reuse previously heard or read material or make up their own definitions.	Monitor the pair work. Join in with pairs where it might be useful, e.g. if they're struggling with the task.
Tell the students to hide the list, then do some more definitions for them. These can be new ones or ones you've already done.	Hands up or no hands up.	You could do this by using translation instead. It would be quicker and less repetitive, but would not recycle the language as much. This is another good example of doing essentially the same task twice, but giving it a twist for extra interest and student focus.
Provide a handout list of about 20 general questions about the topic. Each question should be able to generate longer answers. Work on the first few with the whole class. Model how they can produce longer answers.	Hands up or no hands up.	Modelling is important here. Some students will give concise answers, which means they get less practice in forming original utterances. Allowing the opportunity to extend answers is a good example of "differentiation by outcome", i.e. the faster students have the chance to say more.
Tell them to continue the same activity in pairs. Monitor the work from a distance.	Students work in pairs.	This could be useful down time for you. Take a break, just watch the students at work and enjoy!
Plenary: when it seems that most of the students have completed the task ask them, perhaps in English, if there was anything they didn't understand or anything they wanted to express and couldn't.	Students ask questions, perhaps in English.	After intensive pair work, it's a good idea to have a "release of tension" in the lesson where students can reflect on what they've been doing. It's also useful for you to know what's causing them any difficulty. You could use this time to model any grammatical structures they needed or to hear examples of their answers.

Ways to help generate spontaneous talk

Apart from providing input and the opportunity to develop linguistic skills, it's through classroom interaction with the teacher and other students that spontaneous talk has the chance to flourish. Humour can play a significant role in this regard. When you use humour, students have the impression that conversation is real, so anxiety is reduced (encouraging students to take part) and students are more likely to be humorous themselves, echoing your behaviour.

The way you react to student answers also plays an important role in maintaining conversation. You can use facial expressions, echoing techniques, interested intonation, repeating and reformulating what students say, all with the aim of encouraging students to say more.

The type of skilled scaffolding described elsewhere in the book is also crucial in developing student confidence – carefully selecting and grading questions, while also using the full range of other possible interactions. Asking as many open-ended questions as possible encourages participation and fluency.

Put simply, students are more likely to want to talk if there's something interesting to talk about. This can arise from the intrinsic interest of a text or recording, or from the nature of the activity. With advanced learners the former is the more important; with younger students it's the latter.

Box 9.2: Tech tips

Students, especially those who are reluctant to talk in front of the class, can boost their confidence by using digital devices to record themselves or dialogues with partners.

Voice Record Pro is a popular app for recording good quality audio files and exporting them via email or cloud services such as Dropbox or Google Drive. You can edit and trim the beginnings and ends of recordings, which is useful if students hesitate before they start speaking or don't make it clear when they've finished. They can also read their script scrolling up the screen using a teleprompter such as the **Visioprompt** app while recording with Voice Record Pro in the background. This helps students memorise material for oral assessments.

Yakit Kids is popular with some teachers for practising speaking. Students can take a picture of an object or two, add eyes and mouth and record a voice-over. This is effective for pair work. Students tap each mouth in turn and record questions and answers. You can record clips up to 15 seconds, but using an app like **Videolicious** or **iMovie**, you can put together multiple clips and export them as one so a dialogue could be much longer in length than the 15 second limit.

Soundcloud is a popular means of recording and sharing audio tracks.

Tellagami is an app that allows students to create a short 30 second voice message using an animated, customisable character. This voice message is called a "Gami".

Concluding remarks

No panaceas, then, just lots of TL input and practice over several years. If you don't have the luxury of that amount of time, I'd apply the same principles but based on a much more restricted repertoire of language and topics. There's little doubt that, with lower-attaining students or those who give up learning a language after a short time, setting chunks to memory is an inevitable solution if you want to give students a sense of achievement. Other ways to help students develop some independence include:

- displaying high-frequency language around the classroom;
- having a common TL policy across the faculty;
- giving rewards for TL use;
- creating a non-threatening environment;
- not over-correcting errors, explaining that errors are a natural part of the process of language learning;
- focusing on vocabulary;
- varying seating patterns occasionally, especially where certain pairs are reluctant to speak in the TL;
- making the TL seem the normal means of communication in the classroom.

Chapter 10

Dissecting a lesson: writing

Introduction

Writing is the least important skill in terms of real-life use, but in recent years the increased use of social media, texting, blogging and emails has made it easier to justify making writing a significant focus. When you also bear in mind that writing reinforces the acquisition of other skills, assists memory retention and provides opportunities for calm yet active lessons, it's easy to justify in the classroom. Even so, if your school has an active homework culture, writing is generally better reserved for work outside the classroom since you need to maximise the opportunities for listening and speaking. In this chapter I'll provide a checklist of the wide range of writing tasks at your disposal, analyse in detail a writing lesson, then look at the specific skills of essay writing for intermediate and advanced students, and the skill of summary writing.

Types of writing task

1. Copy-writing from a book or the board to establish simple spellings

This offers effective practice for beginners as they start to process sound-spelling relationships. The act of copying focuses the attention of students on details of spelling, including the new elements of accented letters. It provides quiet time in a lesson and the chance to process something which has been explained or practised just before. Students often enjoy keeping their own record of grammar notes. I wouldn't worry that copying may seem a dull, uncommunicative task; I'd value it for what it does to aid learning. Just don't do it too much.

2. Writing down words spelled out orally

This is the simplest form of transcription. Relating the phonology of a word to its spelling and the physical act of writing combine to help students remember. Close listening is needed together with an attention to written detail.

3. Writing down TL answers to oral TL questions

As we saw in Chapters 2 and 3 this is a natural extension to oral question-and-answer sequences, allowing students to reinforce and recycle previously practised language. Students can write draft answers on paper which can then be handwritten or typed up neatly at home.

4. Writing down TL answers to written TL questions

This traditional task can require complex processing of written language and the ability to write grammatically correct sentences. You can ask students to write either full sentences or note-form answers. The former may seem artificial, but they require more skill with verb usage. By the way, I wouldn't worry about a task seeming artificial if it provides a clear learning gain. The classroom is a place of learning, not the real world.

5. Filling gaps (with options given or not given)

There's a danger of "death by gap-fill" in language lessons, if you aren't careful, but cloze tasks can be used to practise both comprehension and writing. You can tailor them precisely to your class, giving as much or as little help as you want.

6. Writing down corrected answers to false statements given orally

This multi-skill task involves both careful listening, grammatical judgement and written accuracy. You can easily improvise this type of task when working with a written text.

7. Writing short phrase statements or just true/false on a mini-whiteboard

The mini-whiteboard, as we've seen, is a tremendously useful tool, especially since it means you can easily see how well your class is doing as they display their answers.

8. Taking notes from an audio, video or spoken source

This is highly effective and challenging for intermediate and advanced students. Notes can be taken in English or the TL. The former demonstrates comprehension more clearly, the latter requires more written skill.

9. Completing an information grid based on a written or spoken source

Think of this as guided note-taking. You can scaffold the activity by providing more information in the grid, e.g. partly written words.

10. Writing sentences or a narrative based on a picture or picture sequence

This is a natural extension to the type of work described in Chapter 2 and one which allows students to recycle language practised orally.

11. Writing sentences from short notes (e.g. diary entries)

Once again, it makes sense to do this task having done some previous oral work. Students need to remember what was said, then put their answers into writing.

12. Transposing sentences or text from one person to another (changing point of view)

This usually becomes an exercise in manipulating personal pronouns, possessive pronouns and verb forms. For it to be worthwhile there need to be plenty of items in the text to change.

13. Summarising from an English or TL written text

This is a useful task for advanced students, but the downside of using an English source is that students are getting no TL input in the process (apart from consulting the dictionary). Using a TL source text is, in a way, less demanding since some language is given, but it does need to be understood and reworked. The second option seems preferable to me.

14. Dictation

Transcribing words, phrases, sentences or passages from audio or read by the teacher is a high-level skill. If you do it make sure the task is accessible, reinforces previous work and doesn't produce too much error. If it's too hard it's demoralising. Students generally enjoy the challenge if it's fair. Should you choose to count errors, you can make the activity a team game by dividing the class in two and calculating the total number of errors for each team. Paired dictation or running dictation are popular variants (see Chapter 5).

15. Translating into the TL from a written source

See Chapter 7 for more about this. This is usually best done towards the end of a teaching sequence.

16. Translating into the TL from an oral source

This can be a handy task if you keep the English limited to short phrases, e.g. subject pronouns with verbs, and use it as part of a practice sequence or revision, for example.

17. Writing a passage from bullet points, template, frame or mat (e.g. an A4 sheet containing key language)

You can scaffold this type of task as much as you want for your class. It's another useful exercise to set late in a teaching sequence, or for assessment of writing.

18. Synonyms and antonyms

Give a word orally or in writing and the students write down a word with the same or opposite meaning.

19. Completing sentence starters from an oral source

This a handy filler task during a teaching sequence. For example, having done some oral work on a text, you can ask students to hide the text, then give them the start to a sentence they've read. Students must write down the rest of the sentence as they remember it. You can do this in reverse by giving the end of a sentence. This is all easy to scaffold as you can adjust the amount you provide according to the class.

20. Writing poems in the TL

This can be done at any level. Students can write simple calligrammes (words written in patterns to form shapes) and haikus (three line, non-rhyming poems with five syllables in the first line, seven in the second and five in the last). It may go against the spirit of poetry, but you could provide a simple gapped poem where students choose their own words to fill the gaps.

21. Completing a crossword

Crosswords should not be underestimated. They're an excellent source of input, test comprehension and require accurate spelling. You can easily design your own. At the time of writing, the site armoredpenguin.com is an excellent free way to make your own crosswords.

22. Writing for a purpose

This could include letters, emails, text messages, news articles, job applications, reviews, obituaries, diary entries, blogs, dialogues or sketches. If you can supply a real-life purpose to a written task there is the potential for greater motivation as well as the opportunity to refer to specific cultural requirements and writing techniques, e.g. how to sign off a letter or email, use texting conventions and so on.

23. Writing social network messages to a TL speaker or classmate

If your school allows you to do this you can send messages in real time using a phone or tablet, either to classmates or, say, to an exchange class. Even if you don't have the technology or are not inclined to use it, you can pretend to send real-time messages using mini-whiteboards, for example.

An intermediate-level writing lesson

Strictly speaking this is a listening-writing lesson, but the outcome is a piece of writing about the students' school. Begin by telling students that by the end of the lesson they'll be able to write an article or blog which they could share with a student from the TL country. You could also mention that this type of writing is really useful for their exam. Using assessment to motivate always seems a last resort, but it works if you don't overdo it.

The sequence described in Table 10.1 takes between 40 and 50 minutes. Students get to hear, read and write key language multiple times, producing some oral work in the process. It's true that this very structured lesson is largely teacher-led and spoon-feeds the class a good deal but, if the learning outcome is worthwhile, this type of lesson has its place. You can choose to view this as efficient modelling of good writing. The amount of language you provide very much depends on the class in front of you.

Writing an intermediate-level essay (free writing)

One of the harder challenges for intermediate students is to write a short essay to a time limit under exam conditions. Many students perform brilliantly, others seem to fall apart as they panic and fail to remember very much. Let's look first at what's going on when a student has to put together connected writing.

Here is a typical question from a GCSE (intermediate) exam paper in England (translated, for exams from 2018):

> *You're describing your teenage life for your blog*
> *Describe:*
> - *Your favourite pastimes*
> - *Your relationships with your family*
> - *A recent activity with a friend*
> - *Your plans for next weekend*

Table 10.1 Describing a school: writing sequence

Teacher	Students	Commentary
Give students a grid to complete in English with notes. Information included is: type of school, geographical location, number of students, facilities, clubs, subjects you can study, favourite subjects, describe a teacher. Tell them in TL they have 5 minutes to complete the grid in English in note form.	Students complete their sheet in silence.	This gets students thinking about the topic and gives them ready-made information they'll use later in the TL. It's an easy and immediately engaging way to the task.
Ask TL questions about their school which match the points on their grid. Vary the difficulty of the questions. Get other students to repeat answers or give their own.	Students offer answers. Hands up and no hands up.	Make any gentle corrections as required. Some questions will elicit the same answers, others will depend on individual students' preferences.
As students answer, you write on the board gapped versions of the answers in TL. Tell students to take notes, filling in the gaps if they have time. Tell them not to worry if they don't fill all the gaps; they can complete them later. If you tell them the task is to be completed at home they will be extra-motivated to get as much done as possible in class.	Students copy these notes, filling in the blanks as they go along.	The number of gaps you leave depends on the class. Able classes will need bigger ones. Students will be motivated to fill all the gaps so that they don't have to think about it for homework. As you write point out in TL or English any notable written details: "Don't forget that accent", "See how that word is pronounced – say it again after me", "What does it remind you of?"
Display a model version of the school description on the board. Read it aloud, deliberately making the occasional error. Tell students to raise a hand if they hear a discrepancy.	Students read and listen, raise a hand when necessary and correct.	You can make this as obvious or as subtle as you wish. With able classes it may be a mispronounced gender, with others it may be a whole word or phrase.
Hide the text and do an aural memory gap-fill task, i.e. read the passage, leave gaps and wait for a student to supply the next word.	Students raise their hands to supply missing words.	High-achieving classes will supply more than just one word. Very quick students may supply a whole sentence.

Box 10.1: A model of stages in the writing process

1. Planning

In this case the goals of the essay are clear (provided the student understands them since they are written in the TL) and provided by the question. The student selects the most relevant items of information from memory and organises them into a coherent writing plan. Finally, when organising thoughts the student keeps in mind what they've been taught, e.g. "keep it simple", "include opinions", "use at least three tenses", "make every sentence interesting", "stick to the point", etc.

2. Translating

The large majority of students (not native speakers of course) will translate their ideas from English into the TL. This involves turning ideas into English words, then putting them into the TL.

3. Reading and editing

Reading and editing should improve the quality of the writing. The editing process checks that the grammar is right, looks for any problems of meaning and checks that the question has been answered.

Now, when you look at the model above, what can you do to help students carry out the process of writing an essay most effectively? Below is a list of strategies.

- **Teach and review plenty of vocabulary** related to the topics they'll encounter. Lists are provided in exam specifications and text books. Lack of vocabulary is the main obstacle students encounter in the heat of an exam.

- **Focus on high-frequency language**. This means words and chunks that could be used across different types of questions. You'd expect students to be able to manipulate three or more tenses of verbs such as *be, have, do, go, take, play, visit, watch, listen, eat, drink, travel, leave, return, arrive, talk*, and so on. Tell students deliberately to try and work on these verb forms and build sentences around them. In this case they can follow the advice given in Chapter 9: use what you know!

- **Show students examples of questions** so they understand the sort of things they'll have to write about (not a very extensive list in truth). Give students the impression they'll be able to apply what they've learned; there'll be no surprises. Make sure they're well acquainted with the TL instructions and prompt types.

- **Give students plenty of practice at answering questions**, often to a time limit in class or at home. In the early stages you could give access to a dictionary so that students can keep learning and reviewing vocabulary. Later they need to write using their memories only.

- **Model examples of good and poor essays**, giving a close commentary as you read them through. Students' own essays may be a great source of material.

- **Use the "thinking aloud" strategy** whereby you put together sentences on the board, giving a commentary, e.g. "I'm answering the question... I've added a couple of adjectives here to add interest... I've used a linking word and intensifier... I've shown I can write a complex sentence with two clauses... I've shown off the conditional... I've double-checked the gender", and so on.

- **Explain how to plan well**. Even when the question content is obvious, students can be encouraged to brainstorm words which relate to the question. Many students just forget to include lots of words they actually know, so teach them to write lists of all relevant words at the top of their page. These can then be ticked off as they're incorporated into the answer. Explain this is about technique, not inspiration!

- **Show them the mark scheme** (rubric) and how an essay is graded. Get them to grade a partner's work. Stress that there are more marks for writing understandable information than being really accurate.

- **Intertwine essay practice with further written and spoken texts** that recycle similar language they'll have to use themselves. Use narrow reading and listening – tasks like this often come with text books – see Chapters 5, 7 and 8.

- **Use other writing tasks** such as translation into the TL to reinforce grammatical accuracy and recycle common vocabulary.

- **Use sentence-builder grids**. Table 10.2 shows one for French.

By the end of your weeks of preparation you want essay writing to become second nature so that students can produce a good piece of writing when the pressure is on.

Table 10.2 Sentence builder

Je	ne	ai *(have)*	jamais *(never)*	à la plage	avec mes parents
	n'	suis *(am)*	rien *(nothing)*	au tennis	avec mes amis
		vais *(go)*	plus *(no more, no longer)*	la télé	le weekend
		m'appelle *(am called)*	personne *(no-one)*	des musées	le soir
		connais *(know)*	nulle part *(nowhere)*	Eric	pendant les
		regarde *(watch)*	que *(only)*	frères et sœurs	vacances
		joue *(play)*	ni... ni... *(neither... nor...)*	films sur internet	
		vois *(see)*	pas de *(any)*	mes oncles et tantes	
		visite *(visit – a place)*	aucun(e) *(not a single, any)*	au golf	
		télécharge *(download)*			

Teaching advanced-level essays

A major challenge for advanced-level students is to write an effective discursive essay, both as part of the course and to be done under examination conditions to a time limit. For example the A-level examination in England and Wales requires students to spend about an hour writing about a film or work of literature. Essays are graded according to the relevant analytical and critical response, along with the range and accuracy of language used. How do we help students to rise to the challenge of writing effectively to a time limit?

Some teachers like to get students writing essays from an early stage in the course so they become accustomed to the technique as soon as possible. I would rather build up gradually from writing sentences and short paragraphs, to longer summaries and paragraphs, then eventually to fully fledged essays.

As you work through a book or film with students, you can provide worksheets with vocabulary, notes and questions to be answered, along with other written tasks. Students gradually develop a knowledge and language base they can bring to bear when writing an essay. You need to share with students any available mark schemes, then help them acquire good techniques for producing an essay. During this process you'll supply lists of commonly used generic language and idioms for essays, along with any genre-specific language, e.g. cinema terminology. You'll also show examples of effective essays to model best practice – the students' own essays may supply what you need. Some teachers get students to hand in a plan and list of language to be used before they let them write the final essay.

Below is a suggested plan of attack you could give students when faced with an essay title.

Box 10.2 Student guide to writing advanced-level essays

Carefully choose the best title from the options available, anticipating which one will be most fruitful.

Brainstorm any ideas relevant to the title and jot them down at the top of your page – try to focus on about five or six key areas you wish to stress and exemplify from the text or film.

Organise the ideas on the page, perhaps colour-coding them, or circle and link them with lines.

Make a note of any particular phrases or idioms you've memorised and wish to include in the essay.

Keep any introduction and conclusion very brief – they are unlikely to add extra marks.

When writing, avoid telling the story. Make a key point, exemplify it, analyse it and move on.

To assist the reader, imagine you are taking them for a walk; keep holding their hand, don't let go, i.e. use any techniques such as linking words or phrases to keep the reader with you.

Organise paragraphs as follows: PEAL (Point, Exemplify, Analyse, Link to the essay title and next paragraph).

For added style keep in mind rhetorical devices such as the "rule of three" ("I came, I saw, I conquered") and rhetorical questions.

Make every sentence as interesting as possible linguistically, avoiding the simplest turns of phrase, while not resorting to too many hackneyed expressions.

Do a systematic check for accuracy at the end. Reread a few times and look for specific error types on each read through: verb forms, gender, cases (in German) and adjective agreement. Does every sentence make total sense?

To assist students with their approach to planning you could suggest they use a sheet like the one in Table 10.3.

Table 10.3 Essay planning

Nouns	Verbs
Adjectives and adverbs	Linking words/phrases
Complex structures, e.g. subjunctive	Idioms

Essay marking and feedback

Research is unclear regarding how useful correcting essays actually is, but students want to see what you think. At advanced level you'll want to correct in a bit more detail than with younger classes. Too many corrections are likely to be counter-productive, however. Where a student is very error-prone it's better to be a little selective, focusing on major errors which affect meaning, such as verb tense.

One interesting approach is to get students to leave a margin on the right of their page with a note to you about any uncertainties they had while writing. There may be a point of grammar which causes confusion, or a tricky choice of vocabulary. If a student writes a query they're more likely to be interested in your feedback and respond to it. This also allows you to see what students are finding difficult. Some teachers like students to produce a first draft of an essay for comment before they write the final version.

In any case, students improve essay-writing techniques with repeated practice, including writing them in class to a time limit. Don't worry for one moment if the class is writing – it gives you time to do something else. It's one way of making sure your students are working while you're managing your workload.

Writing TL summaries

This is in itself a great multi-skill classroom activity, but is also a feature of some advanced-level exams. Summaries can be written of written and spoken texts. Once you've worked on a listening or reading text with a class, exploiting it in various ways, (e.g. pre-reading/listening tasks, reading aloud, oral interactions including question-answer, correcting false sentences, aural gap-fill, information gaps, grammatical activities with a focus on form, etc.) a natural and more challenging extension of the sequence is to ask students to pull together their knowledge by writing a TL summary of the original source.

A good assessment should ideally reflect classroom practice and this task does so. Teachers have to help students develop their technique, of course. This can be modelled orally, scaffolded with bullet points and practised outside the classroom or to a time limit in class. Students need to learn to identify key points, not to transcribe large chunks, but also not to feel that every item of language needs paraphrasing. They should be as concise as possible. They also need to be familiar with the mark schemes, which reward communication of key points and use of varied, accurate TL. Teachers can use these mark schemes when assessing students' work in the run-up to exams.

Box 10.3: Tech tips

Good intermediate and advanced-level students can create a blog using a free platform such as **Blogger** by Google or their own TL Facebook page. You'll need to check your school's policy on the use of social media, of course. One approach is to ask students to write composition homework on their blog for a few weeks instead of on paper. If they're already producing other work electronically for you they can easily copy and paste it to their blog or page for you and their peers to read what they've written.

Seesaw offers an alternative way for students to keep a digital journal of their writing, with the option of adding other material. Students can add a picture, video, link, note, drawing or file. It also divides them into classes, so they can see each other's work (if you choose). You can approve each piece of work before it's posted and leave comments on work.

Padlet is a popular app that allows students to collaborate by sharing information on a page that all can see. For example, when working on an intermediate or advanced essay, students could contribute their sentences and paragraphs for others to read and use. The teacher can also see what students have contributed. You could ask an open-ended question as a starter or plenary, and have students compose and share answers. In addition, work can be shared with parents. Padlet can also be used to showcase student work or to allow twinned schools to share material in a monitored environment.

The **Textivate** online program is a very fruitful way of practising writing skills in class or at home. Textivate allows you to use pre-written texts or to create your own, tailored to your classes. Exercise types include gap-fill, reordering of sentences, gapped translation and matching tasks. It also has a text-to-speech facility where students can hear any written text spoken. Most of the interactive activities generated by Textivate can be used from the front of the room with an interactive whiteboard. Where appropriate, text boxes and tiles, which can be dragged and clicked, are numbered for easy reference in the classroom. You can get the whole class involved with putting text in order, filling gaps, re-constructing texts, matching vocab, memory games in two teams, playing "Millionaire" and more.

Bubble.us is a web-based tool which allows teachers and students to create simple mind maps. This could be useful if students wish to share essay plans digitally.

Languages Online offers writing exercises of various types, including transcription tasks and gap-filling. It can be used for French, German, Spanish and Italian. Exercises are organised by topic or grammar.

Text-to-Speech sites and apps are an opportunity for students to write out material before hearing it read aloud. There are lots to choose from.

Duolingo, mentioned in Chapter 8, provides opportunities to write accurately at sentence level.

Concluding remarks

Writing is probably given too much emphasis in school courses, largely because of tradition and the continued stress on writing in exams. Effective language teachers must, however, give writing its due place in the scheme of work or curriculum plan. Bear in mind furthermore that many children are more comfortable writing language down than speaking it since they have time to reflect and there is no peer pressure to perform. If, in addition, if you see it as just another way of reinforcing work done in the other skills, it's even easier to justify its place.

Chapter 11

Teaching all abilities

Introduction

Every nation where English is the first language faces a challenge in motivating students to continue studying other languages to a higher level. Students often begin with enthusiasm, then interest wanes during secondary school and many choose to drop languages as soon as they can. Policy makers are constantly torn between the desire to produce more capable linguists and the reality that many don't want to continue or just find language learning really hard. At the time of writing there's a move in England back towards languages for nearly all up to the age of 16, creating challenges for schools that may lack the staffing and recent experience of teaching all abilities to this age and beyond. This is exacerbated by the strong international emphasis on maths, English and science and that in England and Wales research has shown that high exam grades are harder to achieve in languages than in other principal subjects.

In this chapter I'll consider the issue of grouping by ability or prior attainment, and how teachers might do the best for students with lower motivation and/or lower aptitude for language learning. Make no mistake, the range of ability in second-language learning is huge, so that many schools choose to group students by ability at some stage, some from the very start. I'll also look at approaches which might better suit students with special needs and also for high-attaining students.

Grouping by ability: to set or not to set?

The research is not terribly clear on the extent to which outcomes are altered when you group children by ability. In general, it suggests there may be a slight advantage for those in the top group, but there's a disadvantage for those in middle and lower groups, so, if anything, the overall effect *may* be slightly negative. Research needs treating with caution, though, since much of this has been conducted on maths, perhaps because of its perceived importance and the relative ease with which you can measure outcomes. In sum, the research tells us there are better ways of increasing attainment than by putting students into ability sets. Yet a large proportion of schools in England group students by ability in some form. Why?

Progress in both maths and languages involves a steady accumulation of knowledge and skills where understanding the previous step is quite important before you move on to the next. Most teachers feel this to be the case and therefore see teaching mixed ability groups as a challenge or problem. Others, for sound social reasons, prefer mixed ability groups in principle. However, if you believe that acquisition is dependent on giving large amounts of understandable TL, then it makes sense to pitch this at a level appropriate to the ability or attainment of the class. With this in mind, many secondary schools take the view that students' needs are better served when they can move at a pace which suits them.

So why does research seem to confirm that setting is ineffective? Some arguments have been put forward: teachers go too fast with top sets, not allowing knowledge/skills to be embedded; schools assign weaker teachers to lower sets; students in lower sets feel less worthy and behave less well. Evidence shows that lower sets often end up doing low-value tasks, such as filling gaps on worksheets. It's also clear that some students find themselves in lower sets because they have a poorer work ethic to begin with. This is why some schools avoid setting: you end up with all the difficult customers in the lower sets and classes become harder to manage.

In the absence of research about ability grouping in languages specifically, we're left with hunches and the evidence of experience. My own is that ability grouping is desirable in most secondary schools, but that it needs some imagination in its implementation. As always, context is key and it may well be that setting doesn't suit the culture or size of a particular school. The beliefs of teachers may play a role too; it's better if staff believe in the system. If there's a strong culture of academic excellence and a degree of competition, then setting may be appropriate. Whether or not you set, you're bound to be compromising in some way. Keeping groups mixed may mean you're hampering the progress of the most able and not fine-tuning your lesson plans enough to the ability of your classes. If you do set you may initially lower the motivation of the less able.

Here are some ways you might implement ability grouping to make it work most effectively.

- Don't have groups in a simple A, B, C, D hierarchy.

- Have just one top, accelerated group. This may avoid a "sink set" mentality creeping in with the other groups.

Teaching all abilities

- Look at the precise range of attainment in a year group and adjust the pattern of groups from year to year – perhaps there's a persistent small tail of low-achievers who need particular attention.

- Assign teachers to certain groups to make best use of their skills; you can even make sure your lower groups get the teachers perceived to be the best.

- When arranging lower sets, split up more difficult students.

- Make sure there's easy movement between sets; students are often very motivated by the idea of moving up a group; some also request a move down.

- Pack the top sets with more students and make lower sets as small as possible.

- Go out of your way to have high aspirations for lower sets and compromise on standards as little as possible. You have to dispel the feeling among students that they're somehow second-class citizens.

- Make sure that lesson plans and schemes of work are finely tuned to each group.

John Hattie, in his widely read book *Visible Learning: A synthesis of over 800 meta-analyses relating to achievement*, writes (p. 95):

- *Instructional materials and the nature of instruction must be adapted to these specific groups;*

- *Simply placing students in small or homogeneous groups is not enough;*

- *For grouping to be maximally effective materials and teaching must be varied and made appropriately challenging to accommodate the needs of students at their differing levels of ability.*

Some readers may object in principle to any form of grouping by ability because they believe this is a question of equal opportunities or high aspirations for all. In France, for example, grouping by ability is almost unheard of. They may also argue that setting, banding and streaming are a means of selection that reinforce academic and social differences between students. In answer to these views I would reiterate that the opportunities of all may be best served, in most contexts, by arranging classes so that lessons can be pitched at a level which will ensure the best progress.

General approaches to teaching lower-attaining students

I'm going to start by saying that the general principles of language learning apply to nearly all students: exposure to understandable TL, practice, the four skills (listening, speaking, reading and writing), interaction and recycling. With lower-attaining students, however, you have to restrict the diet. The following are some suggestions.

- Instead of trying to get students confident in several tenses, stick to three time frames at most: present, past and future. Be rigorous in selection of language, e.g. do one tense at a time to avoid confusion.

- In terms of vocabulary, cut down the number of words and chunks to be practised, but practise them frequently. Use spaced learning to help memories bed in.

- Make greater use of English and translation. Many students have weak literacy skills in English, so you can play a role in building these, along with their TL skills. In addition, lower-attaining students will have much greater difficulty processing TL input, will get quickly confused and lose motivation.

- Where literacy skills are very weak in English, focus more than usual on phonics (sound-spelling relationships).

- Make everything totally clear and as simple as possible, providing short-term wins for students.

- Explain to students that they will all, at some time, make use of what they're learning. Indeed, they're more likely to use their language than a quadratic equation learned in maths.

- Make sure the assessment system gives a fair chance of success. Exams should be challenging enough, but not too hard.

- If lessons are spaced too far apart, make best use of any homework opportunities to ensure a degree of distributed learning.

- Keep a good balance of four skills, but enhance the role of reading and writing since these involve a lighter cognitive load. Listening and speaking require students to process lots of information on the spot with no time for reflection.

- Be particularly rigorous with your behaviour policy while maintaining a positive spirit in the class.

- Where concentration spans are shorter and memories poorer you need to vary tasks even more than usual.

- Divide lesson plans into shorter sections.

- Be more careful than usual to set written tasks which will produce fewer errors, then be more selective in correcting error.

- Many successful teachers find that more hands-on and visual activities pay dividends, e.g. hand-held flash cards, card-sorting, dominoes and physical activities. But we have to be careful; aspirations need to remain high and you can't fill time with engaging but futile tasks that don't promote the formation of long-term memory.

- Use more short-term testing than average. We know that retrieval tests improve progress.

- Focus more than usual on cultural aspects of the subject to encourage greater motivation. Lower-attaining students are less likely to buy into learning and practising vocabulary and grammar in the abstract.

Adapt your teaching?

Is there a case for adapting your approach more fundamentally for lower-attaining groups? A number of factors may influence your view on this, including any statutory curriculum that may be in place.

The longer-term goals of the students

If you know most of your students will stop doing a language at age 14 years, should you reject the traditional communicative, skill-building approach where benefits might take a long time to be seen? Should you focus on simply maximising the interest value of your lessons and not bother much if the students can't conjugate verbs or make adjectives agree? Would your curriculum even allow you to do this? Alternatively, if you know that some of your students are in it for the long haul and may become quite proficient linguists, should you focus to a greater extent on grammatical form, embedding skills and so on, aware that a small percentage of your students will become proficient and accurate language users?

The timetable

What if you only see your classes once a week for an hour or two? Will students have enough time to build up skills, or might you prefer to abandon this unattainable goal and focus on some situational language and cultural input, which may benefit them for future study or give them a broader vision of the world? If you see your class four times a week you have a much greater chance of getting skills to stick. For many students they do.

The exams they will ultimately take

If you know that nearly all your students will enter for a high-stakes exam such as GCSE, and some will take the language further, this may alter your ambitions straight away. But does this necessarily mean prioritising traditional skill-acquisition over an approach without a strong grammatical syllabus? If you know your students won't do a high-stakes exam, you may be tempted to focus on meaning, culture and enjoyable activity. This might direct their attention to short-term, attainable goals, rather than offering the promise of long-term achievement.

Students with special needs (SEND)

I'm going to paraphrase what a leading specialist in this area, David Wilson, has written for the Association for Language Learning on their website: *all-languages. org.uk.*

> These days most teachers are trained to deal with a range of specific needs, notably dyslexia, since they're found in all schools. In addition, all schools should have a coordinator who shares information and advice about specific students. Part of being an effective teacher is to make sure you're fully aware of every child's specific needs and communicate effectively with the SEND (Special Educational Needs and Disabilities) coordinator.

> SEND is about more than just cognitive and learning difficulties. Other categories of SEND, whether behavioural, emotional and social difficulties, communication and interaction difficulties or sensory and physical difficulties, also have implications for the language teacher. Wheelchair-bound students may be brilliant at Spanish, but must have dictionaries and reference books they need within their reach. An exam candidate with hearing impairment may be entitled to special arrangements in examinations. A group

of students being taught the French greeting *Bonjour* while shaking hands with classmates may contain someone with autistic spectrum disorders who will be distressed by the idea of making physical contact with another person.

David Wilson recalls:

> I once demonstrated the presentation and the practice stages of the unit. A boy, who had formerly displayed behaviour problems, was so intrigued that he insisted on playing the game on his own in several subsequent lessons. However, as I watched him, I noticed that he ignored every spoken French clue in the game. He relied instead on his photographic memory of the locations of the church, post office, café, tourist office, town hall, supermarket, stadium, school, railway station and swimming pool from the presentation phase. Listening comprehension is reputedly the least liked and developed skill in MFL learning. Learners, particularly those with SEN, will compensate for this weakness by enlisting their comparative strengths, in this case spatial awareness. It is always prudent to observe students with SEND at work and to verify their success!
>
> (https://senmagazine.co.uk/articles/articles/senarticles/teaching-foreign-languages-to-pupils-with-sen, used with permission)

Many SEND students do, however, have severe difficulties with literacy and writing, so the natural focus would be on speaking, listening and activity. In addition, students with learning difficulties frequently suffer from poor self-esteem, leading to frustration and disruptive classroom behaviour. You can tackle this by using SEND-friendly strategies. These include using kinaesthetic activities; presenting subject matter in a structured and explicit manner; dividing lessons into digestible "bite-size chunks" with slower learning steps; providing opportunities for "over-learning" key points through a variety of follow-up activities; deploying memory strategies to assist vocabulary and grammar retention; making allowances for shorter concentration spans; showing sensitivity when eliciting student responses; encouraging meta-cognitive – "learning how to learn" – strategies and thinking skills to promote student independence; and dispensing praise and rewards to maintain motivation and self-esteem.

Many of the above strategies apply to non-SEND students, of course, but you just need to deploy them even more meticulously. If you want more information about this topic I suggest looking at specialeducationalneeds.com.

Stretch and challenge

I spent my career teaching students of above-average aptitude in three schools in England, so I'll put forward some thoughts on how to get the best out of the most-able students. Part of being an outstanding teacher is the ability to motivate those often conscientious, high-aptitude students. What I learned comes from my own practice and from watching other teachers at work. Of course, some of the strategies below will apply to all students.

Where do you draw the line between "gifted and talented" students and others? Generally speaking, able linguists have certain characteristics:

1) good powers of concentration;

2) a desire to learn and work hard;

3) an openness to language learning;

4) an ability to discriminate sounds and reproduce them quite accurately;

5) an ability to see patterns in language;

6) in many cases, a strong sense of competitiveness;

7) a desire to be accurate;

8) very good memory skills;

9) high expectations of themselves;

10) high expectations of their teacher.

With these characteristics in mind the following strategies work effectively.

1) Use lots of TL in a structured, graded fashion, resorting to English only for grammar explanation, behaviour issues, occasional translation, some cultural input and some explaining of activities.

2) Do a lot of teacher-led work, especially with near-beginners, maximising high-quality input at just the right pace.

3) Pitch the lesson at just the appropriate level for the group, maybe, on average, above the middle.

4) Make sure the most brilliant are challenged through special attention, letting them give examples and giving them oral and written tasks which allow them to extend themselves, e.g. extended oral answers and lots of creative composition work.

5) Have extra work always available for the fastest workers.

6) Tell them about how language learning works so they buy into your approach. They're likely to have a more sophisticated grasp of these issues.

7) Be very critical of mediocre work when you know it could have been better. They'll almost invariably show off what they can do next time.

8) Challenge their memories with tests and short-term memory tasks such as oral gap-fill based on a text you've been working on.

9) Let them know you're an expert; they like clever teachers. They may want to show how good they can be too.

10) Don't be afraid to do lots of practice examples, e.g. grammar drills, but vary the challenge and give the hardest examples to the best students. Don't bore them by doing too many examples, though.

11) Use no hands up from time to time keeping all students on their toes, but not all the time as you need to let the best show off a bit.

12) Don't play too many games or do gimmicky lessons, or the students will think they're wasting their time.

13) Do plenty of structured pair work as students will use the time well and gain confidence orally.

14) Do some traditional grammar-translation work. They're good at it and enjoy solving puzzles; not too much, though, as it will limit TL input and communication.

15) Use more subtle humour; they get it.

16) Strongly encourage them to do a study trip or, better, an exchange. This will give a huge boost to progress and motivation. Able students often thrive best on exchanges.

17) Occasionally tell them how good they are to boost self-esteem and produce even better work. Not all able children have high self-esteem. Some get particularly agitated before and during speaking tests.

18) Try to make sure they're in ability groups. While, as we've seen, the evidence for grouping by ability is mixed, the most able benefit from being put into separate groups, at least from low-intermediate level.

19) Don't be a slave to the course you're following. Choose activities you know will stimulate. Use those cognitive empathy skills we described in Chapter 1.

20) Use the assessment and examination regime. Able students are highly motivated by examination success and grades.

Specific challenges for able students

French teacher Chris Lowe has provided a menu of challenges for his intermediate and advanced-level students. Their focus was on intercultural understanding. Students can choose from the list for their year group, produce a well-documented project in English and present it for evaluation. As they complete each task they get a stamp on their coffee shop-style reward card. When they get five stamps they receive a special Head Teacher's award. Alternatives to that might depend on the reward system your school has in place.

Below are some examples of Chris's challenges for intermediate students studying French (slightly adapted).

1) Why is the Eiffel Tower a cultural icon?

2) Is there a reason why romance is so often associated with Paris?

3) To what extent are French stereotypes true?

4) Why is France considered a home of culinary excellence?

5) Create a profile of a Francophone country.

They are clearly challenging topics, but within the compass of some students. By the way, these tasks are not limited to a chosen few – all students are entitled to try them.

I like this idea very much. If you prefer the challenges to be focused on language rather than culture it's easy to come up with suitable ideas. High-attaining intermediate students might do a recorded speaking or written task such as the ones below.

- Recorded interview with a native speaker, e.g. a language assistant, teacher or someone in the local community.

- Weekly diary for five weeks.

- Diary of an exchange visit abroad.

- Portrait of someone admired, e.g. from sport, music, film, TV, history.

- Review of a TL film.

- Blog with at least five posts.

- Reading and review of a cartoon book.

Concluding remarks

When looking back at my own teaching of relatively less able students I feel that I gave even more importance than usual to establishing good relationships. I valued working with smaller groups, discovering that they achieved more this way. I did relatively fewer pair or group work activities and made tasks more structured than usual. I simplified the content, using more English within a TL approach overall and did more modelling of tasks than with high-achieving classes. Whereas specific learning strategies (see Chapter 13) more or less take care of themselves with the most able, lower-attaining students need these spelling out more clearly. My main satisfaction, as yours may well be, was being able to build students' confidence and self-esteem so that they felt good about learning a language.

Chapter 12

Pace, questioning and other interactions

Introduction

I don't want to give the impression in this book that there's one best way of teaching languages. Every teacher is different and comes with their own background, personal experience and views about how to get the job done. Indeed, in Chapter 14 I offer examples of some relatively unorthodox, yet successful approaches. Every school is different, which means that teachers work in a wide range of contexts where student ability, behaviour expectations, homework culture, timetabling and so on all vary considerably. But every effective teacher I've seen is able to work at reasonable pace, is skilled with the various interactions they use and knows how to challenge the class in front of them, wherever their starting point may be.

This chapter will look at different types of classroom dialogue: using questions and other types of interaction. I'll look at questioning in detail, showing its distinctive use in our subject compared to others. I'll show how outstanding teachers use a full range of interactions to engage all students, stretching them to the limit.

Maintain the pace

Let me explain why I believe this is important because, in a way, it runs counter to some currently prevailing fashions. For example, teachers are often encouraged to give students thinking time before answering a question. While I can see the point in reflection time (pressure is removed, all students get the opportunity to answer and the most able do not dominate proceedings), understanding and using a second language nearly always requires quick responses. When you listen in real life you don't normally get two chances. If you can train your students to be alert and react quickly, they're more likely to develop the quick reaction skills they need. In addition, if you allow thinking time, the students who don't need it can quickly get bored. Remember that, according to research, the very act of answering questions raises students' academic performance.

Tied in with this is the common preference for no hands up questioning. This comes in two forms. The first is where you ask questions to random students, using a system such as named lolly sticks or even a digital spinner; the second is where you choose a student to answer. I'd argue that the second approach is better since it allows you to use your skill in selecting a student for the particular question you ask. This is a practical and smart way of differentiating between students, while avoiding the same students answering all the time. However, some research suggests teachers find it hard not to favour more confident students, so this has to be avoided.

On the other hand, traditional hands-up questioning allows students to be enthusiastic, and to show off what they know, while providing good models for others. Overall I favour hands-up questioning with occasional use of no hands up. This maintains the pace, encourages enthusiasm and avoids putting students too much "on the spot". As far as the latter point is concerned, let's not forget that language learning is a hard and quite threatening endeavour for students of all levels. Research from psychology strongly suggests we learn more effectively when we aren't anxious, so anything we can do to reduce anxiety in class is to be welcomed. In sum, what I'm advocating is urgency without fear!

Question types and circling

In recent years there's been a focus in schools on using questioning effectively. In professional development sessions question types are analysed, teachers learn about interesting things such as Bloom's taxonomy, and are urged to employ deeper levels of questioning whenever possible.

In language lessons, however, questions are used in a different way. In most cases we don't use questions to explore concepts and help students get to deeper levels of meaning. Questions and other interactions are used mainly as a device to provide TL input and opportunities to practise. This means the questions may be quite shallow and even artificial (*where is the pen?*), but have the important goal of getting students to learn and practise the language. Exceptions to this might be when we question students about grammatical concepts in English or, with advanced students, when we talk about issues at a higher level, using the TL as a means of communication as we would in English.

Table 12.1 lists the different types of questions you can use and how you can do effective question-answer or "circling" (a term mainly used in North America). Below is a hierarchy of questions moving from least to most demanding for students.

Table 12.1 Question types

Question type	Example	Commentary
True/false statement.	*Tom is a cat. True or false?*	Students simply process a statement rather than a question form with its varying sentence structure. Students just have to respond true or false.
Yes/no question through intonation.	*Tom's a cat?*	Students just say yes or no. There's no question form to decode. The intonation of the voice shows it's a question.
Yes/no question.	*Is Tom a cat?*	Students have to do a little more decoding here, but still only have to say yes or no.
Either/or question.	*Is Tom a cat or a dog?*	A little more decoding is required, but students only have to choose between the two options they're given.
Multiple-choice question.	*Is Tom a dog, cat, elephant or crocodile?*	Slightly harder than the above because of the added options.
Question-word question.	*What is Tom?*	The hardest question type since the students can't use much in the input to help them produce their answer.

In doing question-answer work with beginners you can use these questions in order of difficulty, reusing vocabulary repeatedly. Students are happy to go along with the artificiality of the exchange. With higher-level students you could choose question types to differentiate between students, saving the highest-order questions for the most able. This type of circling can be used to work on a single statement.

E.g. *Donald arrived with his friends at the party at 10 o'clock.*

Donald arrived at a party. True or false?
Did Donald arrive at the cinema?
Did Donald arrive with his friends or on his own?
Did Donald arrive at 9.00, 10.00 or 11.00?
When did Donald arrive?
Where did he go?
Who did he go with?

What time did he arrive?
Have you been to a party recently?
Who did you go with?
What did you do there?
What did you eat and drink?

Note how it's useful to personalise questions whenever possible to raise interest. It's often said that adolescents are quite self-focused and that teachers can use this fact to their advantage when planning topics and lessons. Now, there are clearly limits to what you can do with this technique. You don't want to be *too* repetitive, but having a clear awareness of the full range of question types is valuable. The technique allows you to recycle a great deal of high-frequency language, which is fundamental for acquisition.

Types of interaction

Questioning is not the only way to engage in dialogue with a class. It's useful to have a range of different speaking interactions in your repertoire. Your teaching will be less predictable and students may enjoy the variety of approaches. Note that many of these are not just designed for beginners and intermediates. Here's a selection of the many you can use, or which students can use with each other. Remember that just changing the type of interaction can make a task seem different to a class while ensuring repetition.

1) **Choral repetition** (including whispering, shouting, singing). This shouldn't be underestimated. Every student gets to speak without feeling embarrassed. But you must insist on high-quality repetition otherwise it may become routine and undemanding.

2) **Part-group repetition** (small groups, rows, pairs). This adds a simple twist to whole-class choral repetition, but still offers the comfort of speaking with others.

3) **Reading aloud individually or chorally** from text on the board. Choral reading from the board may well be underused by teachers. It's an excellent preface for further oral interactions based on a text, reinforces phonics ability and perfects pronunciation.

4) **Reading aloud** from a worksheet, homework task or text book. Try getting students to read aloud with their fingers in their ears.

5) In pairs, **taking turns to say a different word**, **phrase or sentence** until someone runs out of ideas. The twist of saying "the first person who can't say anything is the loser" heightens enthusiasm just a little.

6) Doing an **information gap task** in pairs, e.g. completing a schedule or diary (see Chapter 4). I can't stress enough how useful this type of activity is. Research scholars emphasise the importance of interacting with other students, and information gaps provide an enjoyable context for this.

7) **Making up true/false statements**, in pairs or for whole class. This is effective when working with written or spoken texts. It's a multi-skill task involving listening, reading, writing and spoken interaction once the statements have been prepared.

8) **Making up false utterances** to be corrected by a partner or the teacher. This is a slight variation on the above. There's something about contradiction that encourages students to take part.

9) **Speaking spontaneously to a time limit** or getting a student to time their partner as far as they can go. Giving students a very precise limit of, say, nine minutes rather than ten can sharpen focus a little. This works particularly well with higher-achieving students who enjoy the challenge of maintaining fluency.

10) **Speaking with a digital assistant** such as Siri, Alexa, Cortana or Google Assistant. If you get students to do this make sure the task is very focused with a set of specific questions to ask, ones which you've tested yourself beforehand. Students should note down answers to demonstrate they've done the task successfully.

11) **Giving a presentation** to a partner or in front of the class. The former is more efficient, but there's something to be learned by having to speak in public. Choose students carefully for this and younger ones will be keener, of course.

12) **Chanting or singing** verb conjugations or vocabulary themes. Recall how anything that makes a task memorable is useful.

13) **Correcting false sentences** made up by the teacher. This is an excellent listening task and source of comprehensible input since students are keen to spot your errors. You can tailor this precisely to your class.

14) **Oral gap-filling** (where you read aloud, leaving gaps to be filled in). We've seen how this can be tailored on the spot to the class. Try doing it once you've worked for a while on a written text (see Chapter 3).

15) **Miming guessing games** (e.g. "mute customer" where one partner mimes items they want to buy from a list and the partner has to guess them). This doesn't produce a great deal of oral language, but is enjoyable and memorable.

16) **Speed-dating** pair work. The simple act of changing partners regularly allows students to recycle language without feeling the task is too repetitive. This works well in the run-up to speaking assessments when there's already a greater sense of urgency on the part of students.

17) **Complex whole-class games**, e.g. Alibi (see Chapter 6). It's worth noting again that these involve a good deal of listening to the teacher so, once again, are an excellent source of input.

18) **Paired dictation**, including running dictation (see Chapter 5). This can be scaffolded with gap-filling. It can be made interactive by requiring listeners to ask for repetition and clarification.

19) Students **asking the teacher questions**. We tend to neglect this aspect so it's no wonder students stumble when they have to ask questions. After running through a question-answer sequence, just tell students to ask you some questions. You can bring humour and thus greater attention to the task by deliberately and repeatedly giving the wrong answer in a dead-pan fashion.

20) **Students acting as the teacher** in front of the class and leading oral work. This is best done once you've modelled the behaviour yourself. Remember that a proportion of your students will themselves become teachers and that the experience of leading a class may even be life-changing for them – in a good way!

21) **Students making a simple request** (*May I go to the toilet? May I take off my jacket? Can you repeat please?*) These can be uttered to simple song tunes. Such phrases are often displayed on classroom walls.

22) Listening and speaking in a **language laboratory** (see Tech tips in Box 12.1). Language labs offer pairing facilities and the opportunity to interact with the teacher.

23) **Reading out numbers**, e.g. when playing bingo or "Countdown", the mental arithmetic game played on TV where students are given a number in the

hundreds, then a selection of small numbers. They have to combine the small numbers by addition, subtraction, multiplication or division to arrive as close as possible to the solution.

24) **Chanting or singing the alphabet and numbers.** This is enjoyed by beginners and some older students too. You can make it interactive by joining in yourself, e.g. saying every other number or letter.

25) Playing **aural anagrams with a partner**, where one person reads aloud an anagram, the partner notes down the letters and has to work out the word.

26) **Describing a simple picture** for a partner to draw. The partner can ask questions for clarification.

27) Taking part in a one-to-one or small group **oral assessment task**. This is an efficient means of assessment when you're short of time for one-to-one tests. Just set up small groups and go round listening in and taking notes. You wouldn't do this for a high-stakes test.

28) Playing **"Chinese Whispers"** (known as **Telephone** in the USA). To keep more students involved you can start the chain from either end of the classroom or even at several points if you have students seated or standing in a circle. Messages can travel simultaneously in different directions.

29) **Practising or rehearsing** for an oral assessment or major examination. When running a lesson like this it's useful to stop proceedings every few minutes to model good answers and give some added impetus to the task. You can even write up words, expressions or structures you wish the students to use in the following five-minute section of the lesson.

30) Taking part in a **formal debate**, a useful activity for advanced students. Students may be unfamiliar with this format so you'll have to explain the role of proposers and seconders. The rest of the class can be involved by taking notes or asking questions.

31) **Presenting and videoing** a sales pitch or news broadcast (see Chapter 4). This requires considerable negotiation between students.

32) Performing a **situational dialogue**, sketch or very short play. These may come from text books or can be written by the students themselves. Younger students enjoy acting out very much.

33) **Role playing**, including parent and child scenarios created by you (e.g. a mother discovers cannabis in her daughter's room), agony aunt (good for

practising modal verbs – *you could, you should*) and crystal-ball gazing (good for practising personality adjectives and the future and past tenses).

34) Making up a story **one word at a time**. This can be led from the front or done in groups once you've modelled the task. This is largely about vocabulary recall and correct use of syntax. When a sentence comes to a natural end a student is allowed to say "full stop" (period).

35) **Accumulation games**, e.g. *I'm going to the market to buy...* Each student has to add a new item to the list, repeating all the earlier ones. You can help this along with a list, and (a small tip) encourage students to associate the item with where the student who said it is sitting. A good class may be able to remember at least ten items. You can give hints by using gesture or mime or pronouncing the first sound or syllable of the word.

36) Simple **transformation drills** led by the teacher (where you say a sentence in the present tense, for example, and the students have to answer using the past or future, perhaps changing another element at the same time).

37) **Substitution drills**. Similar to the above, you give a sentence and the student changes one element of it. These make excellent fast-paced starters, drawing on language used in recent lessons.

38) **Lip-reading** with a partner. This can encourage very careful articulation.

39) **Dice games**, e.g. by rolling dice and, with the aid of a numbered sentence-builder grid, students make up complex sentences in pairs. After a few minutes, they then hide the grid and produce sentences from memory or invent brand new ones. Younger students especially enjoy absurd meaning combinations and may make up amusing examples of their own. See Table 12.2.

40) **Word limit conversation**. You provide pairs of students with a set of simple questions to ask each other. Each answer must have a precise number of words, for example seven for near beginners, 15 for intermediates.

Table 12.2 Dice game sentence builder (French)

1	Je	mange des frites	en cours	tous les jours	pour s'amuser
2	On	danse le tango	dans la chambre	le weekend	avec des amis
3	Amélie	joue de la guitare	sur la plage	chaque soir	en hiver
4	Il	joue de la trompette	dans une cabine téléphonique	de temps en temps	avec son chien
5	Karim	chante en français	dans la voiture	souvent	sans aucune raison
6	Elle	parle espagnol	dans la cuisine	chaque matin	à Noël

Box 12.1: Tech tips

It's possible to collate recordings recorded on **Voice Record Pro** and **Audacity** to listen to, using **Google Classroom**, for example.

Language laboratories have moved on a lot since the days of very unreliable reel-to-reel and cassettes. They can be used to simulate role play and conversational language skills. Listening comprehension activities allow individual students to listen to a digital source such as a live web broadcast, any digital audio file format, a live teacher or student microphone. Students can also do advanced-level listening examinations using the system.

Sanako systems can be installed for wired or wireless use with PCs, notebook computers or tablets. With a wireless set-up students take a tablet and a set of headphones each when they enter a classroom, log on and within three minutes a class is ready in the "virtual corridor" on the teacher's screen. You're available to students via an intercom facility and can discreetly monitor and assist students without disturbing the rest of the class, thus boosting student confidence in speaking in the TL. **SchoolShape** Language Laboratory is a more affordable cloud-based system that allows you to share interactive activities such as gap-fills and comprehension tasks. It has the benefit of a large number of ready-made activities. **Smartclass+** and **Televic** are other laboratory systems.

Concluding remarks

Any excellent lesson has to run at a good pace, where the students are challenged but not given too little time to complete a task. This is one of the hardest skills to master because it all depends upon your judgement of the students' ability and how long you think they'll take to complete each activity. To conclude, below are some elements which are often associated with lessons featuring good pace and interaction. How do your lessons measure up against these?

- You set challenging time limits, but don't necessarily stick to them. You can remind students during the task how much longer they have. It's all about injecting a sense of urgency.

- You check for understanding at various points during the lesson. When you're very skilled you don't need to do this too often as you've developed a keen sense of what's working.

- You avoid spending time on activities that don't take the learning forward, e.g. doing excessive practice examples.

- You ensure prior knowledge is identified to ensure the appropriate starting point for a lesson. You frequently begin lessons by referring back to the previous one.

- Transitions between activities are quick and well-managed.

- You don't get side-tracked.

- You avoid "dead time" during which some students finish a task early and wait while the rest of the class finishes.

- You're prepared to change your plan as you go along, adapting to circumstances.

- You're acutely aware of when boredom might be setting in.

- You're prepared to vary the pace. There are times when you need some reduction of tension in a lesson, when students need to do quieter, reflective activity.

Chapter 13

Moving them forward

Introduction

This chapter will focus on formative assessment, sometimes called assessment for learning (helping students progress), preparing students for summative assessment (tests and exams), homework, marking and feedback. I'll suggest learning strategies to help pupils move forward and do well in exams, along with useful homework tasks. I'll begin by proposing my own rationale for effective marking and feedback.

Mark a lot, mark quickly, build relationships

Marking takes us a very considerable part of a language teacher's working week, although, if it's any consolation, perhaps less so than the lives of colleagues who teach English or History. Most teachers spend too long marking for their own good. Why do we mark? How much time should we spend on it? How should we do it?

My starting point is this: **the main aim of marking is to make sure that students have done their work**. Far more important than feedback is the simple point that students have to do the work in the first place, taking as much time and care as possible. My experience, and it may be yours, is that, frankly, you can't trust some students to do their work properly unless they know you'll be checking it, reading it carefully, correcting it and, yes, in many cases grading it – although I suspect the careful checking is more important than the grading.

Many students want to please you, and one key way they can do this is by impressing you with their written classwork and homework. If you don't mark their work regularly, they'll probably spend less time on it and therefore make less progress. However, you only have so many hours in the week, so you have to mark quickly and not spend too long writing comments. If the alternative is to set less work and mark it more slowly and meticulously, it's a less desirable one in my view. Less work means less TL input, less recycling, less practice and less progress.

So what about making life easier by marking work in class? This is a great idea for some types of exercise, but bear in mind these points. Firstly, the type of task you can easily mark in class (grammar drill, gap-fill, comprehension matching task, etc.) has its limitations and can be easily copied. Some students cheat. Secondly, going through and ticking an exercise in class is a bit routine and boring; you can start classes with something more engaging. This is an argument for checking homework later in the lesson. Thirdly, if you do too much marking in class, some students may start to take their work less seriously because they know you won't be reading it personally. But yes, overall, quick marking in class is worthwhile, recycles language used at home and, crucially, saves you time.

Next, taking books or papers in regularly for marking, or checking work done digitally, is hugely important for you as a teacher. It really shows you how carefully students are working and what they are finding easier and harder. You'll see who the careful, neat writers are, who goes the extra mile by looking things up, who uses Google Translate, who has taken in what you did in class. Furthermore, it's your personal, private means of two-way communication with each student. You can give confidential praise and advice, admonish, build up a rapport and encourage them to want to impress you even more next time. All this helps you maintain good classroom control too, as each student knows that you know them and care about their progress. If you're intimately acquainted with students' written work, you can make subtle reference to it in class, building your relationship further. You can give students an extra glow by sharing examples of their work with the whole class. (Doing this anonymously makes sense too, since there's no potential embarrassment caused to the student in question – "One of us in the room wrote this … isn't it good?")

This is all very well, but marking takes time, I hear you say! In that case, correct selectively, underline or circle errors, then get students to self-correct, use codes, don't write too much at the end and don't bother with practices such as "two stars and a wish" (where you praise two aspects of a student's work then suggest one area for improvement). Two minutes a book or sheet may be more than enough for intermediate students. With experience you learn to go fast. If students know your standards are high, they'll also write more neatly, making your task quicker and more pleasurable. And yes, some teachers like marking! If work is too untidy, don't accept it. If they have to write it out twice, they'll be less inclined to hand in messy work in the future.

Whole-class and peer feedback

Some schools have success in lowering teacher workload by using a technique which has been used for years, namely whole-class feedback. Since many errors in students' written work are repeated and predictable you can deal with them all at once when you hand back work. Typically you'd choose three or four key areas of confusion to run through quickly on the board, possibly getting students to mark in their corrections where needed. Efficiency is the main thing this type of feedback format has going for it. You can deliver the message once instead of multiple times. I believe this should be standard practice, but it should totally replace taking in work to check.

Future-focused discussions can be the most useful when doing whole-class feedback: based on the students' performance, what do they need to do next time? Discussion could identify specifics: things done well that they should continue doing, along with things to stop and start doing. Maybe some suggestions can become whole-class goals, e.g. "Let's see how many of you can include at least five adjectives and adverbs in the next written piece."

Peer feedback is when you ask students in pairs, for example, to check each other's work before it's handed in or after a task is completed in class. This can be the basis of a useful discussion about the task as well as another opportunity to double-check accuracy. This can also be a chance for more able students to help weaker ones.

Are some types of feedback better than others? Table 13.1 presents a summary of types of feedback together with their merits.

Grading

Grading is a contentious issue and you may simply have to apply your school's or department's policy. On balance, I'm in favour of it. High-performing students are definitely motivated by maintaining high grades. To get a lower grade can be a loss of face, which they will want to put right next time. You can even use this to inspire students to better effort and performance. Similarly, even though low grades may be discouraging, you can grade tactically with lower-performing students: when a significant effort has been made, give them a slightly higher grade than the work merited and the students will be delighted, hopefully wanting to keep up that standard. If your grading is "criterion-referenced" in some way (e.g. with letters or numbers corresponding to a level of achievement), so much the better. This means that students have a clear idea of what a grade means in relation to a set mark scheme (known as a rubric in the USA) or in relation to the general standard of the school.

Table 13.1 Quality of feedback

Good feedback	Poor feedback	Commentary
Returning a test or assignment the next day.	Returning a test or assignment two weeks later.	Feedback will seem irrelevant and students will have already forgotten the work they'd done.
Giving immediate oral corrections or recasts where errors hinder communication.	Ignoring errors which impede communication.	If the task is focused on accuracy, errors need to be corrected. With a fluency task it's less important and may be counter-productive.
Choosing two or three points to concentrate on in whole-class feedback. Selecting the salient issues.	Trying to cover several points in whole-class feedback. Spending too long on insignificant detail.	Students are more likely to remember and fix a small number of points explained at once, very clearly.
Including both positive and negative points.	Giving only negative feedback.	The class will usually be more motivated if a feedback session ends on a positive note.
Not writing too much on students' work.	Putting too much red (or any other colour) ink on the page.	Lengthy corrections are too time consuming and demotivating for students.
Modelling good work.	Criticising poor work without showing what good work looks like.	Some students will not understand what they have to do to be better.
Finding useful points to make on good work.	Writing nothing on good work.	You always need to push students to their limit.

What about the old problem, "they only look at the grade, not my corrections?" That's easy to fix. Just allocate a little time for students to make written corrections. Alternatively, if, like me, you find that having students write corrections is an unexciting classroom task, make it part of a homework or save up corrections for a 15-minute session in a later lesson. This forces students to go over earlier work and review language.

Assessment for Learning tasks

Assessment for Learning (AfL) is the process of seeking and interpreting evidence for use by learners and their teachers to decide where the learners are in their learning, where they need to go and how best to get there. Assessment for Learning is also known as formative assessment. In recent years there has been a considerable emphasis on AfL as a means of moving students forward in their learning. Specific techniques language teachers have found useful are explained below.

Learning strategies

One way to help students progress to the maximum is by taking advantage of learning strategies. These are firstly about **making explicit the processes students are already using to help them learn** and, secondly, **exposing them to a greater range of strategies** in order to widen their repertoire and make their learning even more effective. Research generally suggests that strategies should be made explicit and we shouldn't just assume students will pick them up. Should you teach them separately or integrate them within your other teaching? The latter approach makes more sense to me, since it's likely to seem relevant to students.

So we're talking here about integrating strategies into the whole AfL framework (helping students as often as possible to find the best way of working for themselves to make the maximum progress). To make this clearer, in Box 13.1 is a list of strategies under the headings **managing tasks, using what you know, using the imagination, using organisational skills and using resources** (adapted from the site of NCLRC – The National Capitol Language Resource Center, Washington, DC – nclrc.org).

Box 13.1: Summary of Learning Strategies for Students

Managing tasks

Organising and planning: plan the task or sequence; set objectives; plan how to carry out the task.

Think about your own learning: determine how you learn best; create conditions that help you learn; seek opportunities for practice; focus your attention on the task.

Monitor: while working on a task, check your progress; check your comprehension as you use the TL; check your production as you use the TL; are you making sense?

Evaluate: after completing a task, assess how well you've accomplished it; assess how well you've applied the strategies; decide how effective the strategies were in helping you accomplish the task.

Using what you know

Use background knowledge: think about and use what you already know to help you do the task; make associations.

Make inferences and predictions: use context and what you know to work out meaning; read and listen between the lines; anticipate information to come; make logical guesses about what will happen.

Personalise: relate new concepts to your own life.

Transfer/use cognates: apply your linguistic knowledge of other languages (including your native language) to the TL; recognise cognates.

Substitute/paraphrase: think of a similar word or descriptive phrase for words you don't know in the TL.

Using the imagination

Use imagery: use or create an image to understand and/or represent information.

Use real objects: manipulate real objects as you use the TL.

Use role play: act out and/or imagine yourself in different roles in the TL.

Using organisational skills

Find/apply patterns: apply a rule; make a rule; sound out and apply letter/sound rules.

Group/classify: relate or categorise words or ideas according to their attributes.

Use graphic organisers/take notes: use or create visual representations (such as Venn diagrams, time lines, and charts) of important relationships between concepts; write down important words and ideas.

Summarise: create a mental, oral, or written summary of information.

Use selective attention: focus on specific information, structures, key words, phrases or ideas.

Using resources

Access information sources: use the dictionary, the internet, and other reference materials; seek out and use sources of information; ask questions.

Cooperate: work with others, including the teacher, to complete tasks, build confidence, and give and receive feedback. Talk yourself through it: use your inner resources; reduce your anxiety by reminding yourself of your progress, the resources you have available and your goals.

Strategies in practice

Let's look at how you might use strategies, particularly with regard to the teaching of **listening** and **reading**. Remember: this is just about how you help students to use strategies to become better listeners and readers.

How to teach strategies

Research suggests that for strategies to work they need to be applied repeatedly and teachers need to keep re-modelling them to students who may otherwise quickly forget to use them. The list below illustrates one approach to explaining strategies to students.

1) Explain what the strategy is.

2) Explain why it should be learned and applied.

3) Explain how to use the strategy; here, you break down the strategy, or model it in use for students.

4) Explain when the strategy should be used.

5) Explain how to evaluate use of the strategy.

Next, we'll look at how this would work in practice.

Strategies for listening and reading

Listening

- Work out the type of text (conversation, news, etc.).

Moving them forward

- Work out the level of formality.

- Work out the general topic (gist).

- Pay attention to background clues (background noises, background scene if video).

- Think about the tone of voice.

- Make use of facial and body language (if video).

- Seek out familiar words and phrases.

- Seek out cognates.

Students could also raise their hands when they hear a word they recognise, try to focus on the breaks between words and listen for clues from tense and word order (e.g. in German). You can model all these strategies by talking them through during an activity, using language such as: "I would listen through once to get the gist, not get hung up on individual words. Don't worry if it seems hard at first; that's normal. Then, second time through, you can listen out for individual words and understand a bit more." You can subsequently review strategies with them after an activity has been completed with language such as: "How did you find that? Did you listen for cognates? Did it get easier third time through?"

Reading

Let's suppose you've given the short text in French in Box 13.2 to a low-intermediate or intermediate-level class.

Box 13.2: Les Robots

1   Un robot est une sorte de machine spéciale. C'est une machine qui peut se déplacer en suivant les instructions d'un ordinateur. Comme c'est une machine, il ne se trompe pas, il ne se fatigue pas et ne se plaint jamais.

2   Les robots sont partout autour de nous. Par exemple, les robots fabriquent les voitures. Certains sont utilisés pour explorer des endroits dangereux. Par exemple, les robots peuvent explorer des volcans ou la surface des planètes. Certains robots sont utilisés pour nettoyer. Il y a par exemple des aspirateurs-robots.

---

3   Certains robots ressemblent à des humains, mais ils sont rares. On utilise des robots pour désamorcer des bombes. Les drones sont utilisés dans des guerres, mais ils ont beaucoup d'usages paisibles. Par exemple ils surveillent des terres agricoles.

4   Il y a longtemps, les gens imaginaient des robots. Il y a plus de 2000 ans, le célèbre poète grec Homère imaginait des robots en or, mais le premier véritable robot a été fabriqué en 1961 aux Etats-Unis. Il s'appelait Unimate. Il a été utilisé pour aider à fabriquer des voitures et il ressemblait à un bras géant.

5   À l'avenir, nous aurons beaucoup plus de robots. Ils vont faire des choses que nous ne pouvons ou ne voulons pas faire. Ou bien ils vont faire des choses qui sont trop dangereuses pour nous. Ils vont nous aider à lutter contre les incendies, ils nous aideront à combattre les guerres et ils vont nous aider à combattre des maladies. Ils vont nous aider à découvrir beaucoup de choses.

One approach to teaching this text while incorporating strategies would be as follows.

1)   Ask the students in pairs to jot down in two minutes anything they know about robots. This **activates prior knowledge** and **raises interest** in the subject. Quickly get the students to feed back. (This is their first strategy, though you may not choose to mention it yet.)

2)   Tell them you have **a real French article** about robots, which will tell them more about the subject. Read it to them, perhaps asking them to follow the text with a ruler or their finger (depending on the ability of the class). This enables them to hear and see sound-word relationships and gives them a first contact with the text.

3)   Explain they're going to **use a clever second strategy** to help them understand the text. Then get them to **highlight or underline any words they recognise** because they look like English words. Explain that these words are called cognates. **Model how you would go about it, "thinking aloud"** as you do it. Get feedback. Remind them they can do this with any text they read.

4)   Next, so the lesson doesn't become one solely based on talking about strategies, **read out some true/false sentences** in French. Match the difficulty level of these to the class.

5) You can now introduce **a third strategy**. Tell them this is to help them understand the text, then give an example sentence and how you identified the verb in it. To help them understand in more detail, ask students to highlight or underline any words they think are verbs. If they need reminding what a verb is, what it looks like (from its ending) or where they're likely to find it, then do so. Get feedback.

6) **Now do a "find the French/German/Spanish" task**. Give students, orally, about ten English phrases which they have to identify in the text. With less able groups do them in the order they appear in the text and make them as easy as they need to be. The students can write these down (so that they're all busy). Get feedback.

7) Now **make a statement in English and ask students to match it** to one of the numbered paragraphs. Get feedback.

8) Then give the class some **written questions in English** to answer with the help of a dictionary or glossary. This is their **fourth strategy: using resources**. Go around offering help where it's needed. If the class is very well-controlled, students could work in pairs. Get feedback.

9) **Review the strategies students used and find out whether they found them useful**. Remind students they shouldn't use the dictionary too much and can often understand the meaning without knowing every single word. Tell them you'll try these strategies again next time with another article. You might even ask if there are any topics they'd like to read about. You may wish to reflect on how the above approach compares with just handing out a text with questions for students to answer, not just in terms of effectiveness, but in terms of developing active learners and building your relationship with the class.

Testing works

Studies show clearly that short-term tests of various types are effective in moving students forward. They involve retrieval, and research is clear that retrieval improves learning. It's usually best to make sure students know in advance that they're going to be tested. All four skills need to be assessed, either formally or informally, and most students learn from revising for a test. If the test resembles work you normally do in class, so much the better. Indeed, there's a blurry line between a test and a general classroom exercise. This becomes clear when you distribute a handout and students say "Is this a test?" Any classroom and homework is a test of attainment, but if you formalise the activity and tell students "this is a test" it can add an extra level of concentration and motivation.

Homework

The research is pretty clear on the value of well-set homework at secondary school level, and excellent teachers are rigorous about setting appropriate out-of-classroom tasks. If you have poorly spaced out and infrequent lessons with classes, homework is an effective way to provide more input and practice, filling the gaps as it were. Some teachers are attracted by the so-called flipped model whereby students prepare a task at home to be practised in class. Typically this might involve viewing a video about a grammar point so that class time can be used to practise it rather than explain it. I don't find the flipped approach very appealing, at least with younger classes. The traditional model of using homework to reinforce class work is more effective in my view. Why? Firstly, you the teacher are better placed to explain new points to a class, fine-tuning your explanation to the group and individuals within it. A video, although it can be viewed multiple times, can't do this as effectively. Secondly, you can't trust all students to carry out a task at home. If they fail to do it, the following lesson is spoiled. You might argue this applies to all forms of homework, but with the traditional model at least you know the explanation has been given and practised to some extent. You can follow up unfinished work, whereas with the flipped model there is little point in getting students to redo a flipped task later once it's been practised in class.

In my experience effective homework includes:

- writing or recording mini-essays (free writing tasks);

- working on video listening worksheets;

- completing grammar exercises such as translation both ways, sentence combining and gap-filling;

- doing specific tasks, e.g. making a recipe, interviewing a family member (see Chapter 4);

- memorising vocabulary for a test;

- working on an interactive web site or app (on condition that evidence that the work was done can be provided);

- reading comprehension tasks;

- writing or recording a presentation;

- reading and note-taking or summarising.

Above all, students need to know that you take homework seriously, set challenging and often interesting tasks and that you will check it's been done. In terms of your own workload you need to set a balance of work, some which requires you to check it carefully and some which can be marked quickly in class.

Preparing for examinations

There's little doubt that getting students ready for high-stakes tests and exams is a key skill you need to have. You should read the specification (exam syllabus) carefully, know the mark schemes thoroughly and share them with students so they know exactly what they have to do to get the best grades. In addition, you need to make sure students have plenty of practice in the question types they'll encounter since research clearly shows that students get higher scores when they're familiar with the question format. Indeed, teachers also get better at teaching a syllabus over time, which partly explains the phenomenon of "grade inflation".

This can present a dilemma when the style of the exam may not match your preferred way of working. As a case in point, if the exam features, for example, translation into the TL (as is the case for the English and Welsh GCSE) but your inclination is generally to avoid too much translation in class, you could choose to focus on this largely in the final year of the course. The same goes for the techniques needed for coping with speaking tests (e.g. doing role plays or working from a stimulus photo card). Do you need to do such tasks earlier in the course or should you leave them until later? My own inclination would be to leave them until later. Even so, there is some merit in giving students an early taste of exam-style questions to whet their appetites for the challenges ahead.

My concern is that, if you get too focused on exams too soon, you risk either switching students off or compromising your pedagogical principles. In an ideal world the exam assessment would perfectly match your teaching activities, but this is unlikely to be the case. Students certainly benefit from doing "past papers" under timed conditions and you might find that doing these to a strict timetable over a few weeks sees students improve their scores as they do similar questions and reuse similar language.

Box 13.3: Tech tips

Some teachers enjoy using the app **Plickers**. Plickers lets you poll your class, without the need for students to have their own device. You give each student a card (a "paper clicker"), and use your smartphone or tablet to scan them in order to do instant checks for understanding. Students don't require their own device. The data is automatically saved, student by student, at plickers.com.

Socrative is also used for interacting with classes in various ways. There are versions for the teacher and student. You can create tests using multiple-choice or short-answer questions and collate results to reveal how well students are doing.

Nearpod lets you create multi-choice quizzes for the classroom or homework, as well as gap-filling tasks. You can author your own material or use the ready-made resources provided.

You may have access to a **Visualiser** in your classroom, which allows you to immediately display examples of student work or your own models. A **hand-held scanner** or **mouse scanner** can fulfil the same function. **Explain Everything** (mentioned in Chapter 7) can also be used to turn a tablet into a visualiser. There are various ways you can connect a tablet straight to an IWB.

Teachers.io, **Google Classroom** and **Calendar** and **Show My Homework** are examples of tools that allow you to help students organise their homework and share assignments with parents.

Concluding remarks

The distinction between formative and summative assessment has been made clearer in recent years and helped teachers refine their practice. Exam mark schemes and question rubrics are more transparent than they've ever been. Research is also clearer about the value of short-term testing and retrieval for developing long-term memory. But the difference between a test and a practice task is not always clear cut. I've shown that perhaps it's best to think of this in terms of "opportunities for retrieval". In addition, teachers are probably better trained than ever in the details of setting clear goals and moving students on in their learning. Perhaps too much time has to be spent on tracking the progress students make. Teacher workload is high on the agenda, with social media awash with discussions about target setting, homework and marking. It's important to engage a good deal of common sense with regard to these issues and to avoid creating too much work for yourself.

Chapter 14

What makes an outstanding language teacher?

Introduction

In this final chapter I'm going to attempt to distil what you require to be a really effective language teacher while showing, through some case studies, that there's no single way to achieve excellence. I'll list what I consider the key features of an effective language teacher, summarise some important methodological principles, then look in detail at three alternative and somewhat unorthodox ways of achieving success.

What are great teachers like?

Subject knowledge

This comes in three forms: (1) **procedural knowledge**, i.e. the extent to which a teacher can use the TL; (2) **declarative knowledge**, i.e. the explicit knowledge of how the TL works; and (3) **the ability to effectively convey the latter to their students**. In addition, I should mention that knowledge of the TL culture can play a useful role. All these are important but, for me, procedural knowledge is the most crucial, especially when you're working at a more advanced level. If you believe that providing lots of good TL input is important then you'll be a better teacher if you can help provide it effectively. Although we have plenty of other audio and video sources of TL input, you're the one who can fine-tune it best. This requires a good deal of fluency, accurate pronunciation and linguistic accuracy. You'll certainly be hampered if you don't have these attributes. Great language teachers improve their skills and keep their language fresh by reading and listening to as much TL as possible; fortunately this is very easy nowadays.

Expectations

The best language teachers push their classes as far as possible, often working at pace, often expecting quick responses. They correct by giving good models, but not in a way which discourages students. They set work at a challenging level, focusing a good deal on comprehension and skilled manipulation of structure and vocabulary. They give plenty of appropriate homework because they know that maximising the TL input is crucial and that "practice makes perfect". They don't set work needing masses of corrections. They have a clear sense, derived from experience and/or by asking for feedback, of what students find hard. They know when it's important to stress accuracy or fluency. They're very intolerant of lazy work and may simply ask for it to be repeated.

Relationships

These come in all sorts of forms, but the best language teachers establish a relationship which encourages students to concentrate, work hard, want to please and to take risks. This can be through a caring, warm, nurturing style, or by something more formal and business-like. There's no one recipe for this. Teachers may well have a good sense of humour which is appreciated by the class. They praise, but not excessively. They admonish rarely, but effectively. They seldom raise their voice. They have a very good sense of what makes each individual student tick. They share their enthusiasm for the subject and there's a trusting and usually warm rapport between students and the teacher. Crucially they are skilled in all the "micro-behaviours" of classroom management (see Chapter 1 in particular).

Organisation

As in all teaching, the best practitioners plan ahead, have clear lesson objectives, arrive on time, plan lessons well (usually building in a variety of tasks), keep good records, file efficiently, revise from one lesson to the next, probably don't just stick to published course materials, assess regularly, give useful whole class and individual feedback, mark promptly and on a regular basis. They plan homework carefully to reinforce the work done in class. They follow up students rigorously if work is incomplete or behaviour unsatisfactory. They prioritise the important stuff, avoiding being distracted by every new initiative that comes along.

Assessment for learning

They share short- and long-term objectives with classes, respond sensitively to the needs of individuals, have a good sense of what children find difficult (or just ask if they're not sure), use data to set goals – and not just numerical ones. They sometimes explain to students why they're doing particular tasks. Their students should know what they need to do to improve. Teachers may use a mixture of hands-up and no hands up work. They use subtle differentiation during interactions with students. They prepare students thoroughly for tests and exams, while not being scared of doing non-exam-related activities. They use plenty of tests to check how well students are progressing and to show what needs more work.

Sound methodology

Great teachers reflect on their practice. They have some idea of how language learning takes place, believing meaningful TL input is one of the keys to acquisition. They endeavour to create intellectual excitement, whatever the level of the students. They use effective questioning and other interactions, choose input at an appropriate level, find interesting content, know when to use games, pair work, group work, computer-based work, and know how to avoid time-wasting tasks. They think for themselves, based on sound pedagogical knowledge. They can identify which tasks will give the best "return on investment", and believe that practice makes perfect. They have a good repertoire of activity types and explain the language clearly, in a way students understand, but knowing that progress comes more from practice than explanation. Although they work very largely in the TL, they know when this is unproductive. They have a keen sense of when students may be getting bored and when it's time to switch to plan B. They build cultural information into their teaching, sharing with enthusiasm personal anecdotes when appropriate.

Teacher Efficacy

Researchers believe that teacher efficacy has an important bearing on performance and students' progress. Highly effective teachers have a can-do attitude, confident about the extent to which they can bring about desired outcomes of student engagement and learning. Teachers with this attitude:

- take more risks;

- set higher standards for themselves and their students;

- are more likely to adopt innovations and new classroom management strategies;

- question fashionable practices;

- are more persistent and resilient;

- view student failure as a reason to make a greater effort to improve achievement;

- are better at planning and are better organised.

When I trained as a teacher, one of our tutors told us there was no recipe for good teaching, no list of "tips for teachers". I only partly agree with this. There may be no single recipe, but there's plenty of good advice.

Team-workers

No teacher works in a bubble. Great teachers support their colleagues and the ethos of their school. They share resources and ideas, engaging in constructive professional dialogue with their team and their line managers. They also engage with the wider community of language teachers through meetings, social media and professional development opportunities. They take part, wherever possible, in trips, study trips or exchanges. They encourage contacts with students abroad and other native speakers.

Are you a skill-builder or comprehensible input provider?

Part of being a skilled teacher, we have seen, is being able to sort out which tasks are useful and which are time-wasters. How you go about this is bound to depend on your general vision of second language learning.

For over a century there's been a debate between two general schools of thought about how we learn languages. On the one hand, you have those who lean towards the idea of **skill-acquisition**. This means that you think language learning is pretty much like learning any complex activity. You present and practise each little bit, gradually building up the elements in order of difficulty until you achieve some level of proficiency. By this view you'd probably value explaining and practising grammar a good deal, spend time conjugating verbs, teaching isolated words, setting vocabulary to memory, translating and learning by rote.

On the other hand, there's the long-standing **nativist** tradition where second-language acquisition is seen as a unique process in the brain very close or identical to first language acquisition. If you lean towards this view you might talk of comprehensible input, avoid a lot of explicit grammar teaching, do lots of interesting listening and reading, use parallel texts to access more stimulating content, and not force students to speak too soon. You'd avoid grammar drills and translating into the TL.

Skill-builders argue that natural methods are all very well if you're immersed in the language, but that they're inappropriate in school settings where time is so short and shortcuts need to be taken. They question how learning a second language can be the same as learning the first when you already have so much knowledge of your native tongue. Natural approaches, they say, cause confusion in students who want to know how things work. Skill-builders acknowledge that learning a language is hard, but that you can master a limited version of it with common verbs and high-frequency vocabulary. With enough time, many students achieve good results. The skill-building hypothesis underlies the grammar-translation method, the audio-lingual approach and communicative courses with a strong element of grammar progression and practice built in.

Nativists respond by saying that a language is so complex you can't possibly teach every bit and hope students will learn it. They claim that consciously learned language can't become embedded in memory to such an extent that students can speak spontaneously; in other words the idea that you can practise items until they become automatised is a myth. Learning language is not like learning any other skill, otherwise how would young humans pick up language so fast without the cognitive skills adults possess? They add that skill-building methods have been shown to fail so often that the model should be abandoned for most students. What's more, they even claim that skill-building favours the traditionally "academic" child at the expense of the less able, whereas natural approaches are fairer to all since we all possess the same unconscious language acquisition ability. This is why nativists often claim language learning is actually very easy. The nativist hypothesis underlies not only specific approaches such as TPRS (see below), but also communicative approaches that make great use of listening and reading texts.

Where do you stand on this spectrum? It's an important question to answer since it fundamentally affects the general approach you adopt and the specific tasks you choose to do. While there's no clear evidence which of the two general approaches is better, the nearest thing we have to a consensus among scholars is that you need to combine elements of both strands: lots of comprehensible input, but with some "focus on form", i.e. attention to the rules of grammar. I agree with this view, particularly in the school setting. You can, in a sense, have your cake and eat it. In the next section I'll lay out a set of principles based on that assumption. See to what extent they accord with your own.

Key methodological principles

So is there a set of methodological principles which should help lead to maximum success in the classroom? Below is a list we put together for *The Language Teacher Toolkit* (2016), which I wrote with Gianfranco Conti. I wonder how you'd place yourself in relation to these principles and to what extent you'd agree with them. Remember there are few right answers in this field!

- Make sure students receive as much meaningful, stimulating TL input as possible. Place a high value, therefore, on interesting listening and reading, including extensive reading because comprehension of meaningful language is the foundation of language acquisition.

- Make sure students have lots of opportunities to practise orally, both in a tightly structured fashion led by the teacher and through communication with other students. Have them repeat and recycle language as much as possible.

- Use a balanced mixture of the four skills of listening, speaking, reading and writing.

- Promote independent learning outside the classroom.

- Select and sequence the vocabulary and grammar you expose students to. Don't overload them with too much new language at once. Focus on high frequency language.

- Be prepared to explain how the language works, but don't spend too much time on this. Students need to use the language, not talk about it.

- Aim to enhance proficiency, the ability to use the language independently, promptly, in real situations.

- Use listening and reading activities to model good language use rather than test; focus on the process, not the product.

- Be prepared to judiciously and sensitively correct students, and get them to respond to feedback. Some research suggests negative feedback can improve acquisition.

- Translation (both ways) can play a useful role, but if you do too much you may neglect general language input.

- Make sensible and selective use of digital technology to enhance exposure and practice.

- Place a significant focus on the TL culture. This is one way of many to increase student motivation and broaden outlooks.

Case studies

I've already made it clear that there's no single best way to teach a language. Many teachers choose to use approaches that might be considered out of the mainstream, breaking the current "communicative" mould. To avoid giving the impression that I've advocated one style of teaching ahead of any other, I'm including this section of "case studies" to demonstrate there are many different ways of teaching languages. You'll see, however, that these approaches share one thing in common: they all involve providing TL input and opportunities to recycle language. In each case the approach seems to yield very positive results for the teachers who deliver it.

1 A bilingual approach – Michaela Community School

Michaela Community School is a Free School set up in 2013. It's an all-ability school in an inner-city area of north-west London. Its motto is *Knowledge is Power*. It has an above-average percentage of students on free school meals, an indication of its socio-economic context. A significant number of students arrive at the school with literacy problems and around one-third have English as their second language. Students are grouped by general ability at an early stage. Michaela has become well known for its "no excuses" discipline policy, the high achievement of its students and immaculate standards of behaviour. Anyone who visits the school notes how happy and polite the students are, and how well-ordered and aspirational the environment is.

Its team of language teachers, led in 2017 by Jess Lund with support from Barry Smith adopt an unusual way of teaching French. They might sum it up as follows: "Teach like a linguist. Think for yourself, make everything totally transparent, no guesswork, focus on accuracy and ignore orthodoxy." Observers are struck by how much students can do from the early stages of their learning. Below are the main features of the approach they use with near-beginner and low-intermediate students. I've summarised them below following consultation with Jess and Barry.

- Focus strongly on reading from the start (in line with the whole-school policy).

- Focus on one language only.

- Teach from the front; make little or no use of pair or group work.

Outstanding language teachers

- Do lots of fast-paced choral and individual "call and response" activity (e.g. giving a phrase in English and getting the answer back in TL). This is fundamental to the approach.

- Don't use pictures, since focusing on words improves literacy and leaves no room for doubt. Pictures are an unnecessary distraction.

- Use plenty of TL, but don't be dogmatic about it. Students will often ask complex formulaic TL questions in class which they have practised repeatedly.

- Use plenty of translation, especially from English into the TL.

- Place a strong focus on phonics teaching, making links between sounds and spelling very explicit. Spend a lot of time working on letter combinations and how they relate to sounds, e.g. in French, *yeux, deux, feu; boit, noir, oiseau*; and so on.

- Don't worry too much about grading the difficulty of language; expose students to complex language from the start, e.g. beginners quickly learn examples of the subjunctive in set phrases and be urged to use them.

- Get students to read aloud a lot; correct them very clearly.

- Read aloud a lot to the class and be the sole source of listening input, at least in the first 2 years.

- Insist on accuracy at all times.

- Avoid text books and published materials; write amusing texts.

- Include plenty of writing, especially later in each lesson.

- Do no creative writing in the early stages (since students can go wrong too easily).

- Use lots of memory tricks to help students retain language.

- Explain French usage by giving literal translations in odd English: *I have a question important.*

- Make very little use of technology since it's likely to waste time and be less productive. Avoid PowerPoint.

- Emphasise the simplicity of the language at all times. Do this by giving clear rules and using English where needed; leave no room for guesswork or uncertainty.

- Make frequent use of parallel texts so students know at every point what the TL means.

- Do lots of "low-stakes" quizzes, e.g. vocabulary recall.

- No games; a key point for Michaela's teachers is the notion of "return on investment", i.e. which activity will produce the most learning? Games are rejected on principle.

- Use a mix of hands up and no hands up.

- Make lessons fun through the pleasure of learning together, not by doing "fun activities". Develop strong relationships.

I'd pick out in particular the large amount of translation used in order to make everything totally meaningful along with a strong focus on accuracy. Aspects are reminiscent of the Michel Thomas method (michelthomas.com) which you might care to look up online. Traditional immersion-style TL use is rejected since it's deemed to be confusing and off-putting for students, encouraging guesswork. There's little emphasis on creative use of language; even so, a good deal of TL is used and recycled which clearly helps the students remember. The approach is strongly in the skill-building camp and appears to work very well indeed with the students who are used to similar approaches from their other teachers. One message here, therefore, is that a whole-school ethos can affect the methodology of the teacher and the progress students make in language lessons. It's easier to be an outstanding teacher in a school where behaviour standards are high and expectations are clear and consistent.

2 AIM (Accelerative Integrated Methodology)

Pauline Galea is an Ontario Certified Teacher in the Greater Toronto Area working in a Catholic School in Whitby, Ontario. She supplied me with a description of her approach which I summarise here. She teaches French to students aged 9–14 years. Classes receive 40 minutes of French language instruction every day. Pauline is an AIM Certified Teacher and Mentor and serves on the board of directors for the Ontario Modern Language Teacher's Association.

In Ontario, teachers must teach a common core curriculum written and revised by the Ontario Ministry of Education. It places a good deal of emphasis on communication and interaction between students. How teachers deliver the curriculum, however, is a matter of professional judgement.

Evidence of Pauline's students' success is documented in provincial report cards. Most of her students achieve at the provincial standard of 75 per cent or higher. Some are below this standard but none are below a fail. Pauline teaches many students who are on "Individual Education Plans" for various learning challenges. These students are often successful in French language studies and many receive their best marks in French.

So what is AIM? AIM stands for the Accelerative Integrated Methodology. "Accelerative" because students are said to achieve some fluency in as little as 100 hours of instruction. "Integrated" because it uses stories, drama, dance and music to contextualise learning. "Methodology", because it uses specific techniques that have names such as "gesture approach", "pared-down language", "teacher-led self-expression" and "gestural mirroring".

A typical lesson consists of four distinct blocks:

- entry routine;

- whole group, teacher-led activities;

- pair and group work;

- leaving routine.

There's a high degree of structure and predictability to lessons, which fosters confidence and success. The routines become so comfortable that students can often run the class themselves.

Entry Routine

During the entry routine, students are typically taken from their classroom into the corridor where, using gestures, the teacher and students chorally affirm they will use the TL. This creates a psychological mindset and a collective, vocal, physical reminder of the specific behavioural and learning expectations. (*Tout le monde doit parler seulement en français. On traverse la ligne magique et on parle seulement en français.*) Students may also sing an entry rap. Students are expected to speak all the time with the teacher and with each other in unison. By doing this, if a student makes an error, only he or she hears it, and because the language is repeated frequently, the student has an opportunity to self-correct. No student is called on to speak individually in front of the class. Instead students speak together all the time at this stage.

Whole group activities

During whole group (teacher-led) activities, students are brought in close proximity to the teacher, removing any obstacles from between them. The idea is to create and maintain a physically close communicative situation where students are required to focus and actively engage in learning. Teachers lead students through a series of activities which teach pared-down language in various contexts, using word associations, opposites, kinesthetic and oral reviews. Students also work through a series of language manipulation activities including "Choose the right word", putting words in the correct order, matching starts and ends of sentences, TL questions of various types, and retelling stories.

The main focus of the work is short plays that students practise along with songs, grammar raps and word games. They learn to recite entire plays using gestures to support the work. All activities are practised orally and modelled extensively with full participation before activities are handed over to students to complete in pairs or groups. There's little or no explanation of grammatical rules.

In Pauline's class, accountability for learning during the whole group activity is monitored using a *Prof du Jour*. This student sits beside the teacher, and using a class list, records if students are speaking actively, speaking sometimes, not speaking, or absent. Each day, a new student has the chance to be the *Prof*, thereby involving all students in classroom management.

Pair and group work

During pair and group work, students apply any language learned in the whole group activity in small groups. Students work on various oral, reading and writing activities that have been previously modelled. The teacher monitors the groups, joining in where necessary and doing formative assessment via anecdotal notes or checklists.

Groups change at the end of each month so students can have the opportunity to work with different students during the year. At the beginning of each week, a captain is assigned to be group leader. All students are involved in the organisation and routines of the classroom over the year.

Leaving routine

The leaving routine ends the period. Again students speak chorally. Everyone declares that the class is finished, that everyone worked well and spoke well. Pauline leaves the class on a positive note, making all students feel good about learning French.

Throughout the lesson, Pauline also hands out "coupons" to students she hears speaking French. The coupons are an incentive for students to speak only in French and use circumlocution, as opposed to translation, as the first choice in self-expression and communication. Students write their names on the coupons and place them in a box or bag. Coupons are collected for the entire month and are handed back to students at the end of the month so they can count how many they have. They tell Pauline, who records the data for a speaking mark. After the data is recorded, coupons are collected for a prize draw!

The routines, strategies, incentives and activities used by Pauline overcome the students' fear of speaking French, in an attempt to create an environment where students feel safe enough to take the risks needed to express themselves in structured and spontaneous situations.

Interesting aspects of AIM are the near-exclusive use of the TL, the emphasis on choral responses, the low priority given to formal grammar and vocabulary learning, the emphasis on pair and group work and, most notably of all, the stress laid on the use of gesture and the "play" as a key source of input and practice. In practice, studies show many teachers incorporate these features to a greater or smaller extent, with some mixing up the AIM approach with more traditional activities. Teachers who enjoy the play-acting aspects of language learning would enjoy using aspects of the AIM methodology. There is a widespread belief that this approach suits younger learners best.

3 TPRS (Teaching Proficiency through Reading and Storytelling)

Carlyle High School

Carrie Toth teaches Spanish at Carlyle High School, a small secondary school of 370 students in rural southern Illinois. Approximately 60 per cent of students receive a free or reduced cost lunch. The school has a special education programme to support students with learning disabilities or behaviour disorders.

Carrie leads the small language department, using TPRS and TCI (Teaching with Comprehensible Input) to teach the language. The TPRS approach is popular with many teachers, mainly in the USA. Carrie's department motto is: "Retention is key. Engaged students become life-long learners". Results from national testing show that their students exceed expected proficiency levels in nearly every case. The school's switch to TPRS/TCI has seen the numbers continuing with Spanish through to upper levels rise from 30 to 60 per cent. Below are the main elements of Carrie's approach as she described them to me.

- Students read from resources created specifically for them as well as authentic resources, right from the start.

- Beginners pick up and learn structures by doing work based on storytelling. Thereafter lessons include storytelling wrapped in cultural units.

- There are large amounts of question-and-answer work ("circling"). Students begin with simple yes/no answers, then move on to higher-order questions.

- Meaning is established through use of English translation, gesture and images where appropriate.

- Input is 90 to 95 per cent comprehensible, in line with American Council on the Teaching of Foreign Languages (ACTFL) guidelines. Input of 5–10 per cent English is used to clarify instructions, answer questions students don't have the language to ask about, and to give quick grammar explanations.

- There is a strong focus on repetition of structures in new and interesting contexts.

- There is little emphasis on grading the difficulty of language; students are exposed to harder language from the start. The difficulty of language is not "finely tuned".

- There is a good deal of reading aloud to the class.

- Text books are avoided.

- Input always precedes output. Students hear and read the structures in many contexts before they're asked to produce in writing or speaking at the end of the unit.

- Creative writing is encouraged even in the early levels because learning to create with language helps students reach the intermediate level. Mistakes are expected and normal.

- Memory tricks are used to help students remember language.

- Technology is used but only to enhance language learning, e.g. Carrie uses the Explain Everything app to illustrate the class story as it's told, to record audio after class, and to view the "movie" for revision at the beginning of the next lesson.

- Grammar is taught in context rather than in isolation, e.g. if one of the structures is *he/she has*, Carrie will also emphasise that when two people have the same thing in Spanish, you should add an "n"... Each time they learn a new present tense verb structure, then she'll ask the students: *What does it mean if we add an "n"?* So grammar is taught every day, but it's all within the context of the story the class is working on.

- There is a great deal of formative assessment of listening, reading, writing, speaking. If the class has just finished a story unit, they may listen to a parallel story and answer five quick questions about it, retell the story in writing as if two friends had done the things together (changing the point of view via writing), or retell the story to the teacher or to a partner.

- The preferred classroom activities are maximum "return on investment" activities which are rooted in TL input.

- Carrie uses a mix of providing structure to the story and student input into the story's context to keep students engaged and committed to learning the language.

- The aim is to produce fun classes, but where the fun is learning and developing excellent relationships.

You may have noted how certain features echo those used at the Michaela Community School above (the focus on reading and recycling, the lack of tightly graded language, the mistrust of published resources, the use of parallel texts, the importance of good relationships), while others are in stark contrast (e.g. the attitude to error, the use of translation, the lower priority accorded to grammar and the approach to questioning). Overall the approach leans strongly towards the natural acquisition end of the spectrum.

What does a TPRS lesson look like?
Many teachers have taken on board the TPRS methodology to produce excellent, engaging lessons for their classes. In a nutshell the starting point of the approach is that students become proficient by being exposed to meaningful, "compelling" listening and reading input. Grammar is taught, but only, as we saw with Carrie Toth's example, within the context of a story being told or re-enacted. Lots of input is provided before any output is expected, key vocabulary and structures are recycled and a full range of aids are used to help students grasp meaning: pictures, gestures and objects. There are elements of acting out involved, including having students come to the front and dress up. The approach may not suit teachers who prefer a more formal approach to their lessons, since it helps a great deal if you're prepared to act out situations, use mime, props, humour and imagination.

Some elements TPRS has in common with other approaches are: the use of the visual aids, using all four skills, question-answer sequences called "circling", acting out, doing "grammar pop-ups" (briefly explaining and modelling grammar structures and morphology) and using stories as a source of input. Even if you think that TPRS is a poor fit with your syllabus, you might like to include features of it or carry out the occasional lesson in that style.

Here is a typical **lesson plan** (with thanks to Martina Bex):

The heart of a TPRS lesson is the story, which looks like this:

- a character has a problem;

- the character tries to solve the problem and fails;

- the character tries to solve the problem in a new way and fails again;

- the character tries to solve the problem in a new way and finally succeeds.

Many teachers use "scripts", or basic story outlines in order to guide the story and/or to target specific structures (words or phrases). A basic story script might look like this:

- (character) wants (thing); (character) doesn't have (thing);

- (character) goes to (place 1) to find (thing); there are no (things) at (place 1), only (thing 2);

- (character) goes to (place 2) to find (thing); there are no (things) at (place 2), only (thing 3);

- (character) goes to (place 3) to find (thing); there are (things) at (place 3); (character) (decides that s/he no longer wants it, it's too expensive, or buys it and is happy, etc.).

Here is an example story script as described to me by Martina (see Box 14.1):

All of the underlined details in the story are "asked" to the class instead of "told" by the teacher. So you might say, "While Maya was walking, she saw an animal in the distance. What animal did she see?" "Yes, she saw a cow! Maya approached the cow. When she got close to it, what did she think?" "Yes! She thought 'I like cows!'" etc. The language items in bold are the target structures to be practised.

Box 14.1: Maya's story

There once was a <u>girl</u> named <u>Maya</u>, and she was walking <u>to the park</u>. As she walked, **she saw that there was** an animal in the distance. It was <u>a squirrel</u>. **She approached the squirrel**. She thought, "<u>This squirrel is cute</u>. **I'm going to take it with me!**" She grabbed <u>the squirrel</u> and **carried it away with her**.

Then, <u>Maya</u> walked a little more <u>with the squirrel</u> and **saw that there was** another animal in the distance. It was a <u>cow</u>. She **approached** the <u>cow</u>. She thought, "<u>I want milk</u>. **I'm going to take it with me!**" She grabbed the cow and **carried it away with her**.

Then, <u>Maya</u> walked a little more <u>with the squirrel</u> and the <u>cow</u> and **saw that there was** another animal in the distance. It was a <u>fly</u>. She approached the <u>fly</u>. She thought, "<u>This poor fly doesn't have friends</u>. **I'm going to take it with me!**" She grabbed the <u>fly</u> and **carried it away with her**.

<u>Maya</u> walked a little more with the <u>squirrel</u>, the <u>cow</u>, and the <u>fly</u>. <u>She thought, "I'm hungry!" Then, she looked at the animals. She looked at the cow. She said to it, "I'm sorry". Then, she ate the cow.</u>

How does a story turn into a lesson? Martina explains it as follows.

1) **Establish meaning** for the target structures or key vocabulary. You usually establish meaning through translation on the board. Students are encouraged to not repeat the word as you say it; they're told to just listen. Then you give a gesture for the word. Students mimic the gesture as you continue to say the word aloud in the TL several times. Meaning is typically confirmed once or twice by asking a student in English: "What does [TL structure] mean in English?" English is used because it ensures accuracy and is efficient. Images are better in many situations, but are also subject to misinterpretation. Most TPRS lessons target three new structures.

2) **Ask personalised questions** with the target structures. If the structure is "goes to sleep", you might ask, "When do you go to sleep?" "What do you need to go to sleep?" "When is it difficult to go to sleep?" etc. Discuss these questions with your students.

3) **"Ask a story"** using a story script or by spinning a story out of the personalised conversation that you started after establishing meaning. You can bring actors to the front and have them use props to make the story come to life. The story evolves through question and answer, with occasional checks for meaning in English.

4) **Read the class story**. Ideally, you've typed it up so you can project it and read it together. As you read it, use strategies such as circling, checking for comprehension and personalising.

5) **Complete several story activities**. These can include familiar tasks such as hiding the story then doing a retell from memory, answering questions from memory, doing a true-false task or matching starts and ends of sentences.

I recommend that you look at video extracts of lessons on YouTube (TPRS Hangout).

Concluding remarks

So we've seen that classroom methods can vary greatly but usually have aspects in common, notably repetition, significant use of TL and frequent interactions between the teacher and students, or between students. Good relationships are always a necessary prerequisite. In general, however, I'd be wary of anyone who claims to have found the panacea approach to teaching a language! The key factor in the success of any method may not be the method itself, but the skill with which the teacher delivers it. If you're passionate about your methodology and carry it through with aplomb there's every chance it will work. But in general the days should be gone when teachers blindly deliver a package they haven't critically evaluated. Great language teachers develop their own hybrid methodology based on research, observation, experience and a good dose of common sense.

Conclusion

The main aim of this book has been to provide you with lots of different ideas and techniques to support you in becoming an outstanding language teacher. You should now have a greater variety of activities to incorporate in your classroom practice. You need to decide what works for you and your classes, with the focus on achieving the best learning outcomes. Every teacher finds their own particular way of working, but you'd do well to observe as many colleagues as possible, have regular conversations about methodology, read books and blogs, engage with social media and even video yourself at work.

As exam syllabuses change, teachers are constantly focused on the details of the latest curriculum and perhaps spend less time than they'd like re-evaluating the fundamentals of their craft. Pendulums swing and fashions change. Some topics disappear, others come along; tests change, translation goes out of fashion and then comes back; grammar and accuracy gain and lose importance. Despite all this you may have more freedom to be your own boss than you think.

True, classroom time is limited and you have to make sure students are prepared for assessment, but if you bear in mind that much of the language you teach is transferable from topic to topic, you can teach with resources that do not necessarily feature in the syllabus. You can skip over or pay lip-service to topics or tasks you know aren't interesting for students. More important than covering every detail of a syllabus is doing activities which stimulate students and provide transferable language they can use and understand in other contexts. A student who is motivated in this way will go on to value the subject and learn more in the long run. Being a great teacher is about doing what you know works, but being self-critical and modest enough to know that you can always do the job better. Language teaching was an important part of my life for 34 years. It's a great profession and I wish you the best in your efforts!

Bibliography and further reading

Here is a brief selection of books and blogs which either have been referred to in the text or you may find useful. The Stephen Krashen reference gives you a good overview of the comprehension hypothesis, whereas the other books give greater emphasis to the more traditional balance of comprehension and skill-acquisition. The selection of blogs include a similar contrast in pedagogical approaches.

Books

Hattie, J. (2008). *Visible Learning: A synthesis of over 800 meta-analyses relating to achievement*. London: Routledge.

Hunton, J. (2015). *Fun Learning Activities for Modern Foreign Languages: A Complete Toolkit for Ensuring Engagement, Progress and Achievement*. Bancyfelin: Crown House Publishing.

Krashen, S. D. (1982). *Principles and Practice in Second Language Acquisition*. New York: Pergamon Press, also available at sdkrashen.com

Larsen-Freeman, D. and Anderson, M. (2011). *Techniques and Principles in Language Teaching*. Oxford University Press.

Lemov, D. (2015). *Teach Like a Champion 2.0*. San Francisco: Jossey-Bass.

Lightbown, P. M. and Spader, N. (2006). *How Languages are Learned*. Oxford University Press.

Rivers, W. M. (1981). *Teaching Foreign-Language Skills* (2nd edition). University of Chicago Press.

Rogers, B. (2015). *Classroom Behaviour* (4th edition). Los Angeles: Sage Publications.

Smith, S. P. and Conti, G. (2016). *The Language Teacher Toolkit*. Createspace Publishing Platform.

Ur, P. (2016). *Penny Ur's 100 Teaching Tips*. Cambridge University Press.

Bibliography and further reading

Online

ACTFL at actfl.org
Association for Language Learning at all-languages.org.uk
Chris Lowe MFL. By Chris Lowe at chrislowelanguages.wordpress.com
The Comprehensible Classroom. By Martina Bex at martinabex.com
The Language Gym. By Gianfranco Conti at gianfrancoconti.wordpress.com
Language Teacher Toolkit. By Steve Smith at frenchteachernet.blogspot.com
Musicuentos. By Sara-Elizabeth Cottrell at musicuentos.com
Specialeducationalneeds.com. By David Wilson at specialeducationalneeds.com.

Index

Index